Edible (

Vicky Chown
Photography Aloha Bonser-Shaw

bloom
gardening · nature · inspiration

Contents

For Teo
Thank you to Alison and Lucy, my garden mentors

Introduction

The time has come to reclaim the stolen harvest and celebrate the growing and giving of good food as the highest gift and the most revolutionary act
Vandana Shiva, *Stolen Harvest*

Everyone can grow something edible. You might have an enormous back garden that can be transformed into a food forest or a small window box that can be turned into a herb garden – there is always a harvest to be had.

If you only have a small space, fear not. Growing in a compact area can give you focus. Tending to a few pots on a patio or on the windowsill is a worthy practice that reaps delicious rewards. In contrast to a large allotment, a garden, window box or patio are all excellent places to learn to grow, as they are concentrated spaces where you can focus your attention on a few types of plants and really get to know them, expanding on and changing varieties with each growing season.

My method of gardening is very low intensity. Some of my methods may seem controversial compared with advice you might find elsewhere, as I prefer to practise a 'do less' approach. I allow 'good' weeds to grow and let unfussy, useful plants self-sow and flourish, which reduces my workload. My aim is a generous harvest for my kitchen, healthy soil that will work hard year after year and a garden that's full of life.

In this book you'll find my top edible plants and varieties that offer the most bang for your buck when growing in a garden.

Previous page A melon growing
in the polytunnel
Opposite Plants at their peak in
my polyculture garden

In the age of information, there
sure is a lot of misinformation going
around, especially on the subject of
food-growing 'hacks' you see in videos
online. This book is rooted in my
experience as a food grower over the
last 15 years; the trials, the errors and
the successes.

I'm the head urban food grower
(HUG for short) at OmVed Gardens,
which is an educational and
environmental event space and
ecological food garden in north
London. I grow and supply Omved's
no-waste kitchen with seasonal
produce, and I also run the Seed Saving
Network and teach permaculture and
urban food growing.

I am a trained medical herbalist and
foraging instructor and everything
I know about food growing comes from
experience, lots of reading and a few
wonderful, green-fingered friends.
I hope I can pass on some skills and
knowledge and encourage you on your
food-growing journey.

01

Learn
Understand the basics from soil to seed

Why grow food?

Freedom. Growing your own food means freedom. Freedom from plastic packaging and air miles, freedom from having to trudge to the shops for an ingredient and freedom from boring and bland food.

FLAVOUR

Put simply, homegrown food tastes better. Take a packet of fresh basil from the supermarket: while it looks fresh and green, it is often grown in a sterile, indoor environment where its every need is met to create large, 'perfect' leaves. However, it's often mild tasting and watery. A whole packet, whizzed into a pesto, usually only lends a dish a gentle flavour. With homegrown, just a few sprigs of basil bring a huge amount of taste. Is this due to the love and care that went into growing it? Maybe a little. But it's also down to chemicals. Homegrown food is subject to wind, heat, insect attack and disease. This exposure to the elements causes plants to make more phytochemicals – such as the volatile, aromatic oils found in herbs – to protect themselves. This results in much tastier plants and vegetables that are more nutrient-dense.

Opposite Yellow mangetout 'Golden Sweet' in early summer

Most shop-bought tomatoes, cucumbers and peas taste of next-to-nothing compared with homegrown. That is because they are grown for uniformity, easy transportability and shelf life, rather than flavour and diversity. Growing your own means having access to varieties of edibles that are all but lost in supermarkets and even farmers' markets.

SUSTAINABILITY

Homegrown limits waste. You pick what you need, when you need it. You don't always need a whole bunch of parsley, as it is sold in the shops, just a few sprigs for a garnish will do, but what happens to the rest in the packet? It often goes limp or mouldy before it can be used up. There's no plastic packaging when growing your own, no tubs or wrappers to throw in the recycling bin. Any offcuts or unused bits of stem or root can go straight into the compost pile to make beautiful soil for growing yet more vegetables. It's a win-win circular system.

Another benefit of growing your own is that it saves money. Shop-bought fruit and veg can be expensive, especially good-quality produce from the greengrocer or farmers' market. If you're growing using homemade compost, recycled pots and seeds or cuttings obtained from friends and seed swaps, your harvest can cost next-to-nothing to produce – just the love and time you put into it.

DIVERSITY

Small-scale food growing is an artisan craft that leads to the most wonderful colours, variation and flavours on your plate. Seek out interesting, rare, heirloom varieties that are not commercially available to get added value from your vegetable growing.

It's been estimated that 90 per cent of edible crop diversity has been lost in the last 100 years. When looking at the limited produce available in supermarkets and comparing it to the plethora of varieties available from heirloom seed companies, I can believe this. Growing rare, heritage varieties helps to preserve their existence for the future.

Our modern-day, common vegetable varieties are severely limited in terms of genetic diversity. Those that are most intensively grown are bred and chosen for their productivity and harvestability. In short, they are selected to produce maximum profit. Not for flavour, nutritional profile or environmental resilience.

Heritage and heirloom varieties have been passed down through generations, meaning they have stood the test of time and are adapted to their growing conditions. They are genetically diverse, often more resilient to disease and drought, and usually higher in phytonutrients – these are all imperative factors for feeding a growing population in a changing climate. That is not to say that one person's backyard veg will feed billions – but it is a start! If every person in the UK grew just one tomato plant and one basil plant, that would equate to around 150 million portions of tomatoes and basil. That is a mountain of plastic packaging saved and a lot of satisfaction gained.

JOY

On a deeper level, growing and tending to food crops is something rooted in the human psyche. Yet only in recent years has it become more widely recognised that spending time with our hands in the soil can help with all kinds of health problems. Social prescribing is now a thing, with doctors recommending time outdoors and gardening for conditions such as depression. Growing food makes us feel secure, gets us out in the fresh air, provides exercise with purpose and, most importantly, brings us joy.

Ultimately, for me, growing my own food is an act of resistance against corrupt and unhealthy food systems. It is an act of self-dependence and a boost to community resilience. It is a daily meditation, a slowing down, and a better connection with nature and the food we consume.

Polycultures

Humans have worked the land and purposely grown food crops for some 12,000 years. In the early stages of agriculture, humans began to manipulate their surroundings and to farm in a way that reflected nature. They collected seeds and plants, cleared patches of forests and grasslands, and encouraged the growth of certain prized crops for foods, medicines, fibres and animal fodder. They grew a diverse mix of native plants with lots of variation in form and habitat. Their methods would have resulted in something more like a food forest than swathes of single crops. As populations grew, more mouths needed feeding and a method of farming known as monoculture took the main stage.

THE PROBLEM WITH A MONOCULTURE

Monoculture is the practice of growing just one crop in an area at a time, usually perfectly spaced, fed and watered for optimum growth. It produces higher yields and makes it easier to harvest on a mass scale. Essentially, monoculture farming puts profit and yield over flavour, human health and the good of the planet. A monoculture is a risky method.

Opposite A bed of mixed edible plants including rhubarb, nasturtium, Jerusalem artichoke, rose, amaranth and calendula

Take the Irish potato famine of the 1840s. At that time, just one type of potato, the lumper, was grown in Ireland, for its starchy, calorific roots. When potato blight (a fungal disease called *Phytophthora infestans*) spread across the country, this essential crop was devastated, leading to the death of around one million people from starvation and related disease. Growing just one variety of potato meant less genetic diversity and greater susceptibility to disease. But with variation comes resilience. Grow ten types of potato, for instance, and perhaps two or three will have some blight resistance, meaning you will at least get some harvest.

WHY A POLYCULTURE IS MORE PRODUCTIVE

Polyculture is the practice of growing a variety of different edible plants (at least two) in the same area, while also creating habitat for critters, fungi and flora, mimicking the way nature does it. This holistic system has many great benefits, from pest and disease control to bigger harvests from the same, often compact space.

Polycultures can take different forms. They can be tidy and considered, for example, one neat bed of potatoes with a companion plant such as marigolds planted around the edges to attract beneficial pollinators and deter potato beetles. Or it can be wild and sprawling, like an untamed food forest. The latter can make harvesting food feel more like foraging, heading into the undergrowth to treasure hunt for strawberries and nasturtium leaves. I love polycultures, but they do require more time to harvest in comparison with straight rows of neatly spaced lettuces.

The beauty of growing your own edible garden as a polyculture is that you do not have to choose between tidy or wild, flavour or productivity – you can have it all. You can have some neat beds or containers and more wild areas too.

INTERPLANTING

Under the polyculture umbrella, interplanting or intercropping means growing plants together for increased harvest. For instance, I grow shallow-rooted, fast-growing crops such as baby rocket, corn salad and radish around the base of larger, slower-growing plants such as broccoli. This means I can harvest salad five to ten times while waiting for the broccoli to be ready for eating. And rather than keeping the spaces between them neat and weed free, I encourage the right kind of 'weeds' such as chickweed, plantain and dandelions (see Gourmet Weeds, p64). Having this low-growing ground cover helps retain moisture in the soil, meaning the larger plants require less watering and are less prone to bolting in warm weather. (Be sure to spread a thin layer of homemade compost in between salad sowings, to ensure your crops do not compete for nutrients.)

COMPANION PLANTING

Companion planting is a big part of polyculture growing. With a little knowledge of what grows well next to what, you can greatly improve your growing success – some crops will benefit their neighbours, while others will hinder them.

Companion planting can help to deter pests and diseases, encourage beneficial pollinators and pest predators, improve soil texture and nutrient availability, create support and structure, produce cover and suppress weeds. Strong-smelling plants such as garlic, French marigolds and rosemary can help to distract and deter predatory insects such as carrot root fly. Nasturtiums are a favourite food crop for aphids and can help lure them away from beans and peppers.

Some plants have allelopathic qualities, which means they release chemicals that can inhibit the growth of other plants. This is scientifically documented in the case of some plants, such as the hedging shrub cherry laurel (*Prunus laurocerasus*). In the case of others, they have been observed as being bad neighbours. For instance, garlic and onions can inhibit the growth of leguminous crops such as peas and beans.

Right Polyculture bed with peas growing up a support and feverfew and nasturtiums surrounding it

COMPANION PLANT EXAMPLES

This is a brief list of common vegetables with their favourite neighbours and their biggest foes.

Pumpkins and courgettes These create cover to shade the ground for moisture-loving crops but are very hungry, so will compete for nutrients.
FRIEND Sweetcorn, beans, culinary herbs, calendula
FOE Potatoes, brassicas

Peas and beans These legumes leave nitrogen in the soil so are great neighbours for hungry plants.
FRIEND Tomatoes, peppers, sweetcorn, pumpkins, leafy veg such as lettuce, kale and spinach
FOE Onions, garlic

Tomatoes, aubergines, peppers
Tomato plants are heavy feeders so will compete for nutrients with other hungry plants. They benefit from antimicrobial herbs that deter disease and pests. Aubergines and peppers benefit from the same planting companions.
FRIEND Basil, calendula, nasturtiums, chives, onions, garlic, borage
FOE Sweetcorn, pumpkins, brassicas

Garlic and onions These alliums are good interplanting companion plants. Sow them between vulnerable plants to deter insects of all kinds, including slugs, caterpillars and aphids. They may also impart antimicrobial qualities into the surrounding soil, warding off disease.
FRIEND Carrots, tomatoes, peppers, brassicas, potatoes
FOE Peas, beans, asparagus, parsley

Lettuce and leafy salads Try growing strong-smelling plants near to your salads to deter slugs and snails.
FRIEND Peas, beans, carrots, garlic, onions, chives, coriander
FOE Celery, parsnips

Feverfew makes a beautiful companion plant. Its fragrant flowers attract hoverflies and other beneficial insects

Carrots These are prone to carrot-fly attack. Confuse and bamboozle the little pests by planting borders of aromatic herbs around carrot crops.
FRIEND Garlic, onions, chives, rosemary, lavender, French marigolds, tomatoes
FOE Parsnips, potatoes

Soil

Soil is an entire world beneath our feet. All of humanity owes its existence to the fact that Earth is covered by a thin layer of topsoil. Soil is an active, living thing, an ecosystem in its own right.

KNOW YOUR SOIL

Soil science is incredibly complex and could fill the pages of several books. To keep it straightforward I'm covering four basic soil types and how to best work with each one when growing food. There are soils that are chalk or peat based, but these are less common.

Clay Heavy clay soils are common in British back gardens. They are high in nutrients and hold on to lots of moisture, particularly in winter, often becoming waterlogged. They can also bake dry and hard in summer. Either way, plants can suffer and have their growth stunted as their roots struggle to permeate the ground owing to the density of clay. Break up clay soils by adding plenty of well-rotted organic material such as homemade compost. Adding a few handfuls of horticultural sand per square metre, plus a handful of lime (see p133), when you plant up a bed each season also helps to make clay soils more suitable for food growing.

Sand Soil high in sand is light and permeable for plant roots, but is often acidic, has poor water retention and is low in minerals. If you have high sand content in your growing space, add plenty of organic matter in the form of homemade compost. You can also use leaf mould (see p133) to add substance to sandy soils, but it is low in nutrients, so add some slow-release fertiliser such as alfalfa pellets (see p134) any time during the growing season.

Silt These soils are high in minerals and retain moisture but are easily compacted. Silt soils are relatively rare in gardens, but if you suspect you have it, add plenty of leaf mould and fork beds lightly each year at the start of the growing season to aerate the soil.

Loam This is a balanced mixture of silt, sand and clay and is generally considered the best medium for growing. If you have a loam soil in your growing space, you are blessed! Apart from a yearly mulching with homemade compost, little else needs to be added for the perfect growing beds.

A NOTE ON RICH SOIL

You'll notice I mention 'rich soil' throughout the book, particularly in the Grow chapter. Rich soil is simply soil that is full of nutrients. All soils can be enriched by adding homemade compost, well-rotted manure, comfrey fertiliser or other additions (see p133).

THE ROLL TEST

How do you know what kind of soil you have in your garden? The best way to test this is to get your hands in it. Dig down to 10–15cm below the soil surface and take a small amount of soil, then mix it with a little bit of water.

- Clay soil is sticky in texture. It can be easily rolled into a sausage and holds its shape well.
- Sandy soil has a gritty element. You can usually see the sand grains and it does not hold together well when rolled or squashed in your hand.
- Pure silt soils are rare in gardens and have a much finer texture, almost silky. When made into a ball, they should stick together, but crumble when squashed between fingers.
- Loam has a crumbly texture but holds together when rolled into a ball. Like silt soil, it easily breaks apart when pressed.

THE SEDIMENTATION TEST

Another way to find out what kind of soil you have is to use a sedimentation test. All you need is some soil, a jar and some water.

- Fill one mug with your garden soil.
- Place the soil in a large, 1-litre jar. Fill the jar with water, leaving a centimetre or two of airspace below the rim.
- Shake well for a few minutes and let the mixture sit on a level surface for 24 hours. It will separate into layers

of sand, silt and clay. The sand will be at the bottom, silt in the middle and clay at the top. From here you can measure by eye a rough estimate of soil percentages. Anything 50 per cent or more sand is sandy soil, anything 50 per cent or more clay is clay soil and so on. Equal proportions of clay, sand and silt is loam soil.

WORK WITH YOUR SOIL PH

The pH scale rates the acidity of soil from 1 to 14, with 7 being neutral, 1 acidic and 14 alkaline or basic. While some plants have very specific preferences for pH, in general, most plants prefer a neutral pH.

Many plants and vegetables 'lock out' (are not able to use) nutrients in extremes of pH, which can result in poor plant growth, yellowing of leaves and poor production. So it is important to address any pH imbalance, particularly if your garden is growing poorly despite plenty of sunshine, water and added compost.

Acidic soils are relatively common in back gardens and, as mentioned, can have a negative effect on plant health. Some plants such as currants and gooseberries thrive in acidic soil, while others, such as courgettes, do terribly. To work with acidic soil, add garden lime (see p133) to garden beds before planting them up. Use roughly one trowel-size scoop for every square metre of soil and dig in slightly. Wood ash from a fireplace or log burner also has an alkalising effect. Add it to compost piles in moderation – just a few handfuls for every two to three buckets of compostable materials. You can also scatter a handful or two across beds before planting them up.

Alkaline soils are rare, but can occur. If your soil is alkaline, add sulphur – it's available as a garden soil supplement from good garden centres. Using composted pine bark as a mulch is another great way to make soils more acidic. It works especially well with acid-loving plants such as currants and blueberries as it also helps to lock moisture into the soil, preventing berry drop from drought at fruiting times.

THE PH TEST

If you are really keen on getting to know your soil, you can send off soil samples to companies that test for pH, nutrients, soil type and so on. Home-testing kits and electric pH metres are available too. You can also do a simple (though less reliable) test at home.

- Add a handful of soil to a jar. Moisten the soil with a touch of water.
- Add a splash of vinegar. If the soil bubbles, it is more alkaline.
- Prepare another jar in the same way, but this time add baking soda. If it bubbles, it is more acidic. If it doesn't react, it is probably quite neutral.

Clover is a great green manure that adds nitrogen to the soil

GREEN MANURES

All types of soil benefit from constant cover, rather than being left bare. Empty beds are more likely to dry up in the sun, freeze hard and compact over winter, and suffer from leached nutrients in heavy rains. Try growing leguminous cover crops (known as green manures) such as alfalfa or clover in winter and early spring, and in between larger crops such as kale. Dig or hoe these in before they flower (literally break up the plants and incorporate them back into the soil) and leave them to rot down on or near the surface. This helps break up heavy soils, hold together loose soils, and add plenty of nutrients and nitrogen. Green manures are magic.

Seeds

Seeds are the starting point of any successful edible garden. Of course you can buy seedlings from the garden centre, but these are pricey, often sprayed in chemicals, and commercial companies don't stock particularly exciting varieties.

I start nearly all of my plants from seed. It gives me a chance to really get to know the cultivars I am growing, from the first tiny leaves that emerge to the final harvest.

F1 VS OPEN-POLLINATED

Some seeds are F1 hybrids: these have been hybridised by humans and their genetics may not be stable for home seed saving. Essentially, you can save the seed from the parent plant and sow it the following year, but the plant that grows will probably not be the same as the one you collected it from due to genetic throwbacks.

I prefer to only grow open-pollinated seeds: these are seeds that pollinate naturally. Doing this means I can save seed from my plants from one year to the next. Check your seed packets: F1 hybrids should be labelled as such.

SOURCING SEEDS

The best place to get seeds is from your own community. Seed swaps and seed exchanges take place all over the country and seed obtained from locally grown plants are specifically adapted to your local climate and soil type. Seed swaps are happening everywhere: seek them out at community days, local allotments and on social media. There are lots of seed networks and seed guardianship schemes (both in the UK and around the world) where you can become part of a community that grows and multiplies rare and heirloom seeds. Otherwise, try suppliers that specialise in heirloom and heritage varieties – these truly do have more flavour and better diversity than those from run-of-the-mill seed companies.

Seedlings started off under cover in the greenhouse in early spring

Saving 'Blauwschokker' peas to sow again the following year

The seed suppliers and resources I recommend in the UK include the Seed Saving Network, Vital Seeds, the Real Seeds Catalogue and the Seed Co-operative.

STORING SEEDS

Seeds are alive and must be stored in the right conditions to ensure they will grow in the seasons to come. I keep seeds in airtight jars or clip-tight plastic boxes. You can add a silica packet to the jar to absorb excess moisture if your home is particularly damp. Be sure to open the jar every few months to allow new oxygen in.

Sheds and greenhouses are not the ideal place to store seeds as they are prone to temperature fluctuations and damp. Instead, store in a cool, dark place in your home where temperatures and humidity are more stable.

SEED SAVING

Once you start growing edible plants, you can begin to save seed from your most successful crops, sharing them with friends and family and building a deeper relationship with the varieties you grow.

Humans have been selectively breeding plants for thousands of years. Edible plant varieties and people have evolved alongside each other. Saving seed from successful varieties grown in your garden year in, year out can result in more robust crops and plants better suited to your particular growing conditions. See my note about F1 hybrids on the opposite page, as this is important if you want to save seed. I've also listed instructions for saving tomato seeds on p83.

Seed saving is a huge subject and many books have been written about the topic. Just as with growing, each family (and sometimes genus) of plants has different requirements. The subject is a little too dense to dissect here, but if you do want to begin saving your own seed, start with easy things that are largely self-pollinating, such as tomatoes, lettuce, peas and beans. Then if you get seed-saving fever, I recommend doing some further reading around the subject.

Plan
Shape your space, organise your planting and get growing

Understanding your space

Successful food growing is all about getting to know your growing space. The number of sunlight hours it receives, its shady spots and its soil type (see p19) are some of the main observations that will come in handy. Once you know your space, you can move on to the fun bit: planning how and what you want to grow.

LIGHT

Sun, sun and more sun is the key to growing abundant edibles. This is a hard pill to swallow for those of us who grow in shady spots. But not all is lost: there is still a harvest to be had from gardens with limited light – you just need to adjust what you grow and how you grow it.

Most home-growing spaces, whether a patio, large garden or windowsill, have at least a few hours of shade when buildings or trees block out the sun. Observe how the light enters your growing space, not just once but throughout the seasons, as light levels change when the sun is higher in summer and lower in winter. Note where the sun rises and sets and see what areas get the most direct light and which get most shade.

Usually plants are categorised according to whether they need full sun, part sun or shade. Full sun generally means they require at least six to eight hours of direct sunlight per day, part sun means between four and five hours, and shade means anything less than two or three hours per day. You may find it useful to sketch your space and write down how many hours of sunlight each area gets.

Most fruiting plants, such as cucumbers and tomatoes, require lots of sun to produce well. If you have a south-facing garden or balcony, you are one of the lucky ones! If your spot is shady and receives as little as three hours of direct sunlight per day, focus on veggies that are grown for their leaves, such as lettuce, rocket and corn salad. Growing upwards is also an option to maximise access to light.

SPACE

Assess your available growing space; plants are a bit like goldfish – they often grow to the size of their environment. If you only have a window box or a few small pots, you'll struggle to grow huge things like pumpkins. But bush tomatoes, chillies, spring onions and culinary herbs will thrive, as will cut-and-come-again salad crops.

Patio gardens and even balconies with large pots may support bigger veg such as vine tomatoes, potatoes and courgettes, but note that edibles in pots need lots of sun, water and fertiliser to produce well.

Growing on a windowsill, small patio or balcony may not seem ideal owing to space restrictions, but it offers some benefits over growing in the ground. Windowsills and some sheltered balconies tend to be slightly warmer than many gardens as they are tucked in close to buildings, absorbing their heat and giving plants an extra boost. They can also be great for avoiding disease as they are off the ground. There's been many a year when almost every allotment grower I know has lost their entire tomato crop to fungal disease blight, while all the balcony growers have revelled in masses of sweet cherry tomatoes. This is because blight is a fungus that overwinters in soil and becomes airborne at a low level, infecting plants growing in the ground.

That said, if you are growing on a tenth-floor balcony, you may find some plants struggle because of exposure from cold winds. And while a sunny windowsill is great for growing pots of basil and bush tomatoes, even they can get too hot at the peak of summer and need protection from direct rays, as well as extra watering.

Fenced or walled gardens, particularly those in city and urban areas, provide a few degrees of extra warmth, creating

a microclimate that is usually sheltered from gusts and harsh frosts, meaning there is less chance of losing veg to the cold or wind.

If space is a limiting factor in your food-growing journey, choose varieties that can be trained to grow upwards – cucamelons, achocha, nasturtiums and even squash can give huge harvests from just a few square metres of ground/pot space if allowed to grow up a trellis, wall, stairs or balcony. You may be surprised by how much food you can produce in a small, urban garden.

Where to grow

Start by working out what kind of soil you have (see p19) and then consider how you want to incorporate food into your space. You could simply plant a few perennial food crops into borders and have a few pots for herbs and salad leaves. Or you could dedicate a sunny area to annual veg crops, making a defined space for them. Or you could do both!

Whether you are growing in containers, raised beds or straight in the ground, most soils will need improving. Ideally you'll have an active and productive compost pile (see p51) producing plenty of compost that can be incorporated into the areas in which you are planting. If not, you can buy some. Small 50-litre bags of peat-free compost are available from garden centres, but can be pricey. If you have a large growing space, 'Dumpy' or 'Ton' bags of peat-free compost are available from some large gardening-goods suppliers and, even with the cost of delivery, often work out to be much better value for money.

RAISED BEDS

A raised bed is an enclosed, solid frame that can be filled with soil/compost above ground level. It can be constructed straight onto the ground (soil or grass) or onto a hard surface such as a patio. It looks smart and 'purposeful' and is easier to weed (compared with a border) as its walls block grass and weeds from edging in.

Raised beds are a good choice if you have soil that's often waterlogged as they sit above the natural soil level and encourage drainage. They are also a great way to improve the soil in a concentrated area – it's much easier to add amendments (see p133) to a smaller, controlled raised-bed area than the entire garden.

What to grow Pretty much anything that can be grown in open ground can be grown in a raised bed. But if you

Raised, circular beds made with Cor-Ten steel

only have space and materials for a few beds, it may be best to reserve them for delicate, tender plants such as lettuce – raised beds make it slightly easier to manage predatory pests like slugs, as you can surround the beds with protection (see p147). Raised beds are also great for root crops as the soil stays light and uncompacted because it is never walked on.

Construction tips You can make raised beds cheaply from a variety of salvaged materials, including scaffold boards, pallets and pallet covers, bricks, paving slabs and even logs.

They can be any size, from a 30cm wide and deep border edge around a patio to a huge 3m-long (or even 10m-long!) growing bed. The trick is to keep them less than 1.5m wide – that way you can always reach the centre from either side without having to walk on the soil.

If you're looking to create a raised bed on a hard surface, it will only be as deep as the soil you add into it, so you either need to build it with high walls or ensure it is deep enough for the plants' root systems. The minimum depth of soil for healthy plants grown in raised beds on a hard surface is around 30cm, though most plants would love more.

Filling raised beds requires some planning as you need to source enough organic material. If you have lots of homemade compost, you can fill them half and half with garden topsoil and homemade compost, or even fill them all with homemade compost if you have enough.

CONTAINER GARDENING

Not all gardens grow in the ground and not everyone has a garden or allotment. A garden is what you make it and you can use whatever space and equipment you have to hand.

Growing in containers is great for so many reasons. Containers are portable, so you can move them in and out of the sun, or bring them inside when the weather gets cold to prevent perennial crops from succumbing to frost. They are also good for maintaining certain conditions for the plants you are growing, such as for blueberries, which prefer acidic soil.

Some plants, including culinary herbs, tomatoes, peppers and salad leaves, thrive in pots; others, such as carrots and other root crops, can struggle. This is because they grow long, hair-like taproots that go in search of water and nutrients. When the taproot hits the bottom of its container, it stops growing, which can result in stunted roots. However, there are round varieties of carrot and smaller root crops such as radishes that do well enough in containers.

A young tomato plant potted on in its new home

and extra fertilisers and mulches compared with plants in the ground.

If you're recycling containers, ensure they have adequate drainage holes – you can drill holes into plastic containers. Aim for five to ten holes 5–7mm in diameter for a standard-sized bucket. Plants do not like to sit in water, so pots must be free-draining.

GROWING IN THE GROUND

The traditional method of vegetable growing is, of course, in the ground, straight into the soil.

Pot-growing tips It's important to choose the right-size container for the plant you are growing. For instance, basil does well in large yoghurt pots for its entire lifespan. Cucumbers, on the other hand, need a pot that can hold at least 15 litres of soil – you're looking at a bucket or large plastic storage box. Always check the mature growth size for each vegetable before planting in its final container.

You can use pretty much any vessel to grow edibles, but remember that plant roots can't reach and explore to source water or nutrients in the way they can in the ground; they are reliant on what you provide. To produce abundantly, pot-grown food requires more regular watering (pots can dry out very fast during summer)

I generally reserve ground beds for larger crops such as courgettes and pumpkins, which often trail along the ground, growing up to 3m in length. Once your edibles are in, be sure to keep the edges well weeded of grass and other unwanted plants, as these will quickly make their way into the centre if not kept in check. The best thing for this is a half-moon tool: a spade with a semi-circle shape and a sharp edge. If you don't have one, simply use a standard shovel to cut away wayward edges.

If you're planting in a mixed border of ornamentals, choose your edibles carefully. Sunflowers are a fantastic edible and ornamental plant, tall and cheery. And amaranth puts on a beautiful display. It's also tall, with striking flower spikes. Both are best planted at the backs of borders so as not to overshadow smaller plants. Some amaranths, like callaloo, are bred for their edible leaves, others are grain amaranths, grown for their nutritious seeds. Bear in mind, while nearly all amaranths are technically edible, some are grown purely for ornamental purposes and may have bitter and tough leaves or seeds (and they may have been sprayed with toxic chemicals). It is best to select varieties bred specifically for the veg garden and grow them from seed. If you let them go to flower, they will drop seeds everywhere and become a most welcome and tasty weed.

Construction tips Pre-existing garden flower beds will do just fine. If you're creating a new growing bed for edible crops, select a sunny area (full sun is preferable) and mark out the size and shape of the bed. It doesn't have to be a rectangle: circles, spirals, triangles and so on are a little different and equally as effective. Dig out any grass or weeds to a depth of 30cm, making sure to pull out any roots left behind. The excavated soil and plants can be composted. Dig the soil over with a fork to loosen it and incorporate any amendments needed before planting – most garden soils will need additional compost or manure to support happy, healthy crops (see p19 for soil types and p133 for additions).

Fruit tree laden with greengage plums

Amaranth's edible leaves and colourful flowers

NO-DIG BEDS

No-dig beds preserve the structural and nutritional profile of the soil because they are never turned over with tools. Instead they rely on the help of worms and microbes to manage soil structure and provide aeration. No-dig beds are easy to start and maintain, and well worth trying.

- Select an area in full sun. This can be straight onto bare soil or on grass. Mark out your bed size. Remove perennial weeds including dock and brambles, as these don't decompose easily. Annual weeds and grass can be left in place.
- Cover the marked-out area with a layer of cardboard (make sure there's no sticky tape on it). This excludes light and prevents anything from growing. Dampen the cardboard with water to soften it.
- Cover the cardboard with a 10–15cm layer of compost. Plant your seeds or seedlings directly into the bed straight away. The root systems of the plants will find their way deep into the soil and the cardboard will rot down and suppress the growth of grass and annual weeds.
- Once the first growing season has passed, simply treat your no-dig bed like any other garden bed – add a layer of mulch in the autumn and/or spring and plant it up year after year.

HUGELKULTUR BEDS

Hugelkultur beds are fantastic! They are essentially living compost-growing beds, consisting of logs and other compostable materials heaped up in a pile or trench to form a mound or hill that's then covered with topsoil. The materials then slowly decompose, releasing nutrients and heat as they do. The technique has its roots in Germany and is centuries old.

It is a fantastic way of using waste materials that can be found around the home and garden, such as logs, leaves, cardboard, garden and grass clippings, as well as kitchen waste. You can create hugelkultur beds on top of the ground with no digging at all or use one as a foundation for a raised bed.

At the core of a hugelkultur bed is wood. The primary decomposer of wood is fungi, which contain web-like structures known as mycelium. These filaments permeate the composting hugelkultur pile, helping retain water and nutrients in the bed. You won't need to add further compost for at least a few years.

- Choose a sunny spot. Any size bed is fine, but I recommend around 1–1.5m wide by 2m long.
- If you are building your hugelkultur bed on a grassy or weedy surface, do one of two things: dig out the turf/weedy soil to a depth of around 30cm, or place a few layers of

cardboard directly on the grass/ weed surface followed by 5cm of woodchip/compost. Doing this helps to suppress weed and grass growth. If using the cardboard method, water the cardboard until it is sodden before piling on other materials.

- In what will be the centre of your pile, lay down logs with a circumference of 20–50cm (the smaller the beds, the smaller the logs). It is best to use logs that were cut a few months or even years ago, as these will be beginning to rot down already. If you only have access to freshly cut logs, don't worry – they will rot down over time. Avoid using evergreen logs or laurel as these are slow to rot, contain antimicrobial plant chemicals (not helpful in a living compost pile!) and can suppress plant growth. Instead, choose logs from deciduous trees such as lime, beech or oak.

- Add a layer of thinner branches and twigs, aiming for a depth of 30–40cm. These will allow the air to flow within the pile and help the other layers to continue composting down.

- On top of the twigs, add 5–10cm of partially rotted compost, if you have it. If not, a few layers of damp cardboard will suffice. This helps to prevent the pile from drying out.

- Water the pile to get moisture to its core.

- Add a 10–15cm layer of leaves, hay or straw. Water this layer until it's sodden. At this point you can also

The layers of a hugelkultur bed, with logs and branches at the bottom, then green cuttings and compost. This will decompose slowly generating heat and nutrients

pile on any turf you may have dug out from the base.

- Next add a 10–15cm layer of grass clippings, green garden clippings and raw, vegetable-based kitchen waste.

- Finally, add a 15–20cm layer of compost – either homemade or shop-bought is fine. And *voilà*! Your bed is ready to plant up.

CROP ROTATION

Bugs and diseases build up in beds throughout the growing season. Crop rotation is the practice of growing specific groups of annual vegetables in different spots each year to help reduce the build-up of crop-specific pests and diseases in the soil.

For example, to reduce the risk of carrot root fly overwintering in a bed and attacking your carrots next year, simply do not grow carrots in the same bed two years running. For similar reasons, brassicas, alliums and tomatoes should not be grown in the same bed within a three-year period. Bear in mind that some edibles that may not seem like the 'same' crop can in fact belong to the same family and be affected by similar pests and diseases. These include turnips and kale (both *Brassicaceae*), as well as potatoes and tomatoes (in the *Solanaceae* family), and onions and garlic (*Alliaceae*).

Another benefit of crop rotation is that some plants complement others if grown after one another. Legumes, for example, fix nitrogen in the soil. If planted in the same bed the following year, heavy feeders such as pumpkins and tomatoes will appreciate the nitrogen they leave behind.

Keeping on top of this can get a little tricky if you are growing in mixed beds and interplanting, as you may have lots of different families in one bed. The main thing is to take note of any pests and diseases each year. If one appears that is specific to a certain family, such as beet leaf miner, do not grow beets or related vegetables such as chard in that bed for a few growing seasons in order to 'starve' the pest.

Ideally, and if you have the space, leave a four-year gap before growing a particular crop in the same location again. If space is limited, at the very least allow a two-year crop rotation. It is a good idea to plan your garden and draw up a crop-rotation map so that you remember where you planted things in previous years. Families that should be rotated are *Brassicaceae*, *Alliaceae*, *Solanaceae* and *Fabaceae* (legumes, such as beans and peas).

Sweet red pepper 'Semorah'

Planning your plot

We gardeners are dreamers and eternal optimists, always planning for the growing year to come. Every year we learn a little more through our mishaps and convince ourselves that the next growing season will be bigger, better and more productive, and it can be, with a little planning.

A PLANTING SCHEDULE

In all my years of growing food, the thing that surprises me the most is that no two years are the same. An early frost or a wet summer can massively affect what you'll be harvesting from month to month and year to year. For this reason I plan my garden *loosely*.

One area that I do plan well is my sowing and planting schedule. This is so that baby plants can be planted out when conditions are optimum. A late frost can decimate plants that like warmth, such as courgettes and cucumbers, and slow down everything else. Of course, you cannot control the weather and sometimes late frosts, high winds, hail and torrential rains happen with little warning. The best thing you can do is make provisions to protect them.

Each plant in your garden has different needs for optimum health and abundant harvests. If you are new to

Module-sown salad seedlings ready to plant out

Elephant and standard garlic ready to plant

growing, get to know what plants you already have and what plants you want to introduce to your growing space. Write down a plan for each one making a note of some key points.

- When to sow/plant out
- The plant's ideal position/sun requirements
- When/if to feed
- When/if to prune
- How much space the plant needs
- When to expect the harvest

A PLANTING PLAN

If you are new to growing edible plants, try introducing just a few fruits or veggies to your growing space and focus on getting to know how to grow them well rather than spreading your attention between lots of different crops that require different growing conditions and care. See the Grow chapter on p54 for inspiration.

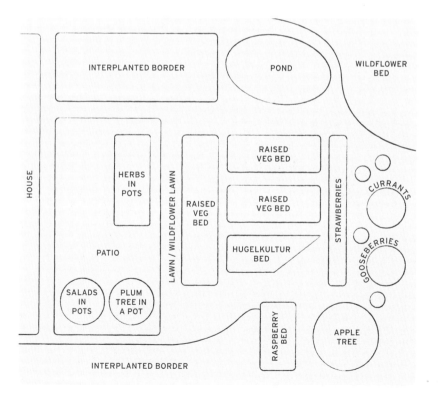

JOBS FOR THE YEAR

Keeping a note of what needs to be done helps you do things at the optimum times. Here are some of my annual jobs to get you started.

January

Hold off on cleaning up until spring as leaves and dead plant matter make habitats for insects, amphibians and all kinds of life forms. Raking and clearing beds can disturb them and expose them to the elements and predators.

- Rest, plan your gardening year and start perusing seed catalogues for things you would like to grow.

February

The days are starting to lengthen but the temperatures are usually too cold to sow direct or even in a greenhouse. Sunny windowsills come in very handy at this time of year, often becoming jungles of baby plants.

- Start off fruiting annual plants that have a long growing season, such as tomatoes and aubergines. Do this indoors under grow lights, on a sunny windowsill or in the greenhouse in a heated propagator.
- Sow peas, onions from seed and a few salad leaves indoors, to be moved into the greenhouse as soon as they germinate.
- Chit potatoes.
- Plant out rhubarb crowns.
- Winter prune apple and pear trees.

March–April

This is when the real work begins. The buzz of spring is in the air and the garden usually grows faster than we can keep up with!

- Continue sowing fruiting plants such as tomatoes, peppers, aubergines, courgettes, French and runner beans and cucumbers indoors.
- Sow cold-tolerant plants like radishes, peas, beetroots, spring onions and rocket direct in the ground or outdoor pots.
- Transplant seedlings from seed trays to individual pots.
- Plant out chitted early and maincrop potatoes.
- Plant out onion sets.

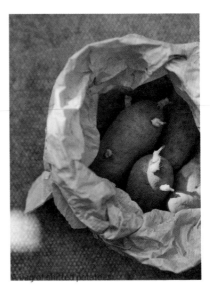

A bag of chitted potatoes.

May–June

By now the weather is warming up and most crops will tolerate being sown in a greenhouse or cold frame.

- Sow squash, courgettes, cucumbers, and French and runner beans in the greenhouse.
- Continue successional sowings of salad crops and peas.
- Start hardening off seedlings and young plants that are still indoors, such as tomatoes, peppers, beans and cucumbers.
- When the temperatures are forecast to be in the double figures day and night for at least two weeks, plant out seedlings and young plants that were growing indoors.
- Harvest salad leaves, young beetroots, radishes, broad beans and early peas.
- Pinch out tomato plants and feed weekly or fortnightly.
- Earth up potatoes.

July–August

The mad rush of sowing and transplanting begins to slow down in summer and you can start to relax and reap the harvests of your spring efforts. This is the time to sow crops that will grow through winter.

- Continue successional sowings of lettuce, leafy greens, radishes, beetroots and carrots.
- Sow winter and spring crops like broccoli, cabbage and kale.

- Sow green manures.
- Harvest tomatoes, cucumbers, courgettes, beans, summer squash, beetroots, peas and peppers.
- Harvest garlic and onions as their leaves start to brown.
- Cut back any leggy herb plants.

September–October

The last abundant harvests are in autumn, with huge pumpkins now ready and, if you're lucky, tomatoes still fruiting. Now is the time to prepare the garden for winter.

- Continue harvesting tomatoes, peppers, aubergines, carrots, beetroots and leafy greens.
- Allow pumpkins to cure on the vine, but bring them in before harsh frosts.
- In September, you can still sow spring cabbages and brassicas.
- In September, sow green manures.
- Dig in summer-sown green manures.
- Mulch beds for winter protection.

November–December

This is the time to nourish the soil, cut back and tidy, and sit back and reflect on the year's highs and lows.

- Dig in autumn-sown green manures.
- Sow hardy broad beans.
- Plant out garlic and hardy onion sets.
- Spread mulch on any empty beds.
- Prune dead or dying plant material.

Sowing seed

There's no one rule that fits all for seed sowing. Each plant has different requirements. Your seed packet will provide some specifics and you'll find further information in the Grow chapter on p54. Here are some tips to ensure a good start.

COMPOST

It is best practice to use seed compost for sowing seeds. Seed compost is finer than general-purpose compost and has been heat treated to kill weed seeds. It contains a good mix of nutrients to give baby plants the best start. I never use peat-based composts and prefer the coco coir-based seed compost.

SEED TRAYS

You can be creative in sourcing seed trays. For example, recycled fruit punnets are a good option. Just make sure there are some holes for drainage and you space out your seeds according to the instructions on the packet.

Some seeds are better started off in module trays. These are trays that have separate compartments for each individual plant. I tend to plant most things in module trays as they allow root systems to develop and ensure minimal disturbance when the time comes to transplant. Brassicas and legumes particularly don't like having their roots disturbed.

If you're growing peas or sweetcorn, root trainer trays work well. These have deep, narrow compartments that encourage deep, strong roots. You can use toilet rolls for this too. See p70 for full instructions and a picture on p42.

WATERING

It's important to keep seeds and seedlings watered correctly. A general rule of thumb is that the soil should feel damp at all times, but water should not visibly pool when the soil is pressed. Soil needs to be kept damp enough to activate seeds to germinate. But overwatering can cause seeds to rot before they even sprout. Once seedlings are up, damp conditions can lead to a fungal condition known as 'damping off', which can kill your whole crop. For this reason it is important to allow good drainage – use pots with holes, and never allow pots or trays to sit in water.

TEMPERATURE

Most seeds require warmth to germinate. Cucumbers and peppers, for example, need warm soil to break their dormancy. Sow these in a heated propagator or on a sunny windowsill. Other plants – salad greens, brassicas and peas – don't require as much heat. These can be sown in early spring in an unheated greenhouse or directly in their final growing spot once soil temperatures warm up in mid-spring.

Sowing peas in loo rolls. For instructions see p70

SOWING UNDER COVER

I generally start seeds off under the protection of a greenhouse or indoor space for a few reasons.

Pests Seedlings are delicate little things and starting them off under cover gives them a chance to toughen up and develop crucial plant chemicals that deter pests and diseases.

Optimum temperature Greenhouse and indoor temperatures are easier

to regulate. Most seedlings are frost sensitive and a cold night can wipe out a whole tray of plants. Warm temperatures (as long as there is adequate light) produce bigger, happier, healthier seedlings.

Head start Sowing under protection gives some plants an early start. This is important for those with a long growing season such as peppers and tomatoes.

SOWING DIRECT

Most plants are happy to be sown directly in the soil, in the same way that you would sow in pots. Root crops like carrots and radish do not like to have their roots disturbed and do much better sown direct. When sowing direct, be sure to remove any weed seedlings first or your veg plants could get shaded out. Prepare your soil in the bed by breaking up any large, hard clumps on the surface. You want a fine soil for sowing seeds. Protect young seedlings from slug, snail and bird attack.

HOW MUCH TO SOW

We are all guilty of getting over-excited at the beginning of a new growing year and one thing all gardeners do at least once is over-sow seeds. You may want to plant 20 teeny-weeny tomato seeds – why not? If all of them germinate and grow on well, you could end up with 20 huge, 1.5m, sprawling plants. So before putting seeds in soil, check how big the plant will get. If you do over-sow, you can always give away the extras.

Potting on and planting out

Potting on is the process of repotting seedlings to a larger pot. This is usually done to allow them to grow bigger and stronger before they are planted in their final growing spot. Planting out means transplanting your small plant to its final outdoor home, be it a pot, raised bed or in the ground.

TRUE LEAVES

When a seed grows, it sends out 'seed leaves' (cotyledons). These are the first leaves that pop up and are part of the seed embryo itself. In some plants these are long and thin (such as onions); in others, such as brassicas, they are heart-shaped. As the seedling grows, it sends out 'true leaves', which look much more like those of the mature plant. Most plants can be potted on as soon as they develop one or more sets of 'true leaves' and you feel they are robust enough to be handled.

HOW TO POT ON

From their growing trays or modules, seedlings can be potted on into 7–9cm pots filled with fine potting compost – either one bought from a garden centre or homemade compost that has been sieved in a riddle. If seedlings have been grown in module trays, simply pop the whole plant out of its module and pot on. If grown in pots with multiple seedlings in the same container, carefully lift seedlings out using a chopstick or the fine end of a teaspoon before potting on.

Once potted, leave them under cover indoors or in the greenhouse.

PLANTING OUT TIPS

Some plants don't need potting on. For example, lettuce and peas can usually go straight from their seedling tray into their final planting place.

Planting out like this is for plants that are not too cold sensitive. Keep an eye out, though: if any frosts are forecast, protect plants with some horticultural fleece, a cold frame or a cloche.

Heat-loving plants such as tomatoes, peppers and squash benefit from a period of prolonged protection from the cold and can only go outdoors when all possibility of frost has passed – usually from mid- to late spring.

If you have an excess of nettle clippings around the time that you plant out hungry plants such as courgettes or tomatoes, try placing a shallow layer of the cut-up leaves at the bottom of the hole you are planting in. The leaves will rot down, providing veg plants with a slow-release fertiliser.

I've listed spacing guidelines in the Grow chapter under some plants (see p54).

Protecting plants under cover

At different points in their life cycle, your plants may need protection from the elements. This is mostly when they are seedlings or when they are being 'hardened off', which means acclimatising to life outdoors (see p57). If you do not have access to any of the things outlined below, a sunny windowsill or some grow lights over the dining table will provide protection for at least a few plants.

Greenhouse A greenhouse gives you dedicated space to sow seeds and protect seedlings from cold temperatures and some pests and diseases.

Polytunnel A polytunnel maximises your growing space and opens up many growing possibilities. It often has space to grow bigger plants in the ground as well as a bench area to start seedlings off. It is usually more economical than a greenhouse and you can even build your own. There are tons of videos and tutorials online showing how to do this.

Cold frame At the other end of the scale, a cold frame can provide just enough under-cover space to protect plants if frost or hail is suddenly forecast. It's a structure with a clear top (and sometimes sides) and is simple and easy to make with some bricks and a sheet of glass or clear plastic. Even a few large, clear storage containers with lids can act as temporary cold frames.

Cloche A cloche offers protection to one plant or a few smaller plants. These can be made of netting to protect plants from pests, or plastic to help insulate against cold temperatures. You can buy them, but plastic bottles with the ends cut off to create mini greenhouses also work.

Horticultural fleece This is a lightweight sheeting made of polyester used as a kind of blanket to protect plants when cold weather strikes. It is handy as it folds down small for storage and is easy to pull out and cover plants with for short periods so as not to lose crops to cold weather. The downside is that it is made of plastic and very fragile, so can break up in windy conditions, leaving microplastics in the soil. Natural wool fleece covers are available, but these are also fragile and need to be handled with care. The great thing about natural wool fleece is that once it is holey and no longer usable as fleece, it can be used to protect plants from slugs, as mulch, or even added to compost as it will biodegrade.

Plants out of place (weeds)

So-called 'weeds' are often just plants out of place. Of course there are plants you will want to control or eradicate completely, such as bindweed and dock, which quickly take over and outcompete edible crops. But there are also delicious dandelions, wild spinach and chickweed, which not only taste good but also benefit the biodiversity of your plot.

The single most useful thing I have learned in my gardening journey is to identify what things are when they are tiny babies. That way when you spot a 'weed' popping up in the middle of your tomatoes, you can work out if it is friend or foe. If it is a useful plant, instead of throwing it on the compost, you can move it to the edge of a bed where it won't crowd out edible crops.

When I have time, I like to create 'oddball' beds — entire patches of the garden made up of random mixtures of plants where all the plants that are out of place can live out their days. Some things grow better with each other than others, so get creative, see what works and enjoy the mayhem and magic of a slightly more wild bed.

An oddball bed of wild and self-sown salad leaves, flowers, herbs and 'weeds'

Building structures

I love to build supportive and protective structures in the garden from natural materials. I start building in mid-spring, making supports for peas and protective cages to shield brassicas and young plants from pigeon attack. I create more as the season goes on, providing vertical supports for climbers and even squash (which can be trained to grow upwards to save ground space). By summer, the structures are barely visible under the lush green growth of heavily fruiting beans, cucumbers and tomatoes. As well as being useful, twiggy structures add architectural interest to the veg garden.

Young pea plants supported by canes and protected by a tent made of netting

CHOOSING MATERIALS

Natural materials such as birch and hazel branches make beautiful structures. The lengths of wood are called 'bean poles' and 'peasticks' (see pictured on p48). Late winter is the best time to source these as the trees are in dormancy. If the wood is not completely flexible, soak it in a water bath for a few days before using. You can either buy poles from a reputable supplier or harvest prunings from your own plants or that of a neighbour (make sure you get permission before taking loppers to anything that's not in your garden). It's possible to use lengths of fresh willow, but note that these root and grow if pushed into the ground – you may end up with baby

Low cages protect strawberries from squirrels

willow trees growing in your veg bed! Always ensure the wood is fully dried out (for a few weeks) before putting it in contact with the soil.

If your structure is going to support a plant as it climbs, choose your base accordingly: use stronger, thicker poles for heavier plants. Runner beans, for example, are very light but grow very tall so need long poles; squash can get very heavy so you need to make sure your structure is robust enough to support the plant when it's fruiting.

MAKING CAGES

I use twiggy cages to protect plants from bird attack (pictured on p46). They look a lot nicer than netting, though they won't protect your plants from small pests such as butterflies and aphids.

Take a few long, straight, flexible poles and push the ends of each one into the ground or pot, forming a semi-circle around the plant. Bend the other ends over the plant and push them into the soil to create a series of crossing arches. For added protection or support, use bushy twigs (hazel and hornbeam work well) to fill in any gaps and stop birds from landing and munching on leafy veg.

Removing the leaves from lengths of hazel. Twiggy branches like these are great for creating protective cages and vertical supports

MAKING NETTED FRAMES

You can use any type of pole to create a frame to drape protective netting over. Before draping the netting, cover any pointy stick ends with tennis balls (cut small holes in each one) to stop the sharp points from damaging the netting and to prevent injury. You can also recycle plastic bottles (cut in half) for this purpose. The draped netting can be secured at the edges with logs or tent pegs.

The structure you make can be as simple as a few poles pushed into a ring around the plant. Or you can create tent frames (pictured on p47). Poke in the poles so they are facing each other and secure them together at the top with string before covering with netting.

MAKING SUPPORTS FOR TALL PLANTS

Tomato plants can get very heavy with fruit towards the end of the season and those tied to one cane may buckle and snap under their own weight. I like to build a tripod to support them, as well as for peas and beans.

Poke in three poles to form a triangle around each plant (pictured top). Tie the poles together at the top with string (pictured middle). Take another long length of string and create a cage around the poles in a zigzag pattern (pictured bottom). No matter which way the tomato leans, it will have support and its fruit-laden stems will not snap.

Composting

A garden is only as good as its soil, and composting is key to soil health. The benefits of making your own compost are endless and, while it may seem daunting, it can be as simple or as complicated as you make it.

Pre-made compost bin I generally recommend against traditional shop-bought plastic bins as I find they have limited air circulation, and they get hot and dry out quickly. But they are an option if space is tight. If you're in the UK, check what your local council offers, as standard plastic bins are subsidised in some areas. You can spend very little or an awful lot on a compost bin. They offer varying degrees of insulation and weather protection for your compost. Some specialist 'hot compost' bins allow you to compost things such as meat and animal waste (which you shouldn't add to an open compost pile or regular bin). They keep the compost hotter and at a more even temperature, meaning they create compost faster. You still need to manage your waste ratios (see p52) and turn the contents to keep it aerated.

Homemade compost bin You can create a compost bin out of recycled wood, chicken wire or pallets. You are essentially making a pen to hold the waste that will eventually decompose.

A three-sided bin with an open top is ideal. Leaving the front of the pile open allows better access for digging and adding waste, though a removable 'door' (a piece of wood will do) keeps the compost pile a little tidier. Leave the top of the structure open to allow the air to flow, but cover loosely with some cardboard, a large piece of wood, or tarpaulin if the weather is very wet and your compost is becoming sticky.

Once you get the hang of it, you may find composting addictive! In which case you could (if you have space) graduate to a classic three-bay compost system. The first bay is for undigested organic material. Once this is full and has rotted down a bit, it gets turned into the next bay, which is for partially digested organic material. The third bay is for the final product: the black gold itself.

Bokashi This is a compact, caddy-style composting container you can keep in the kitchen. It uses active bran to decompose food waste. It's an option worth exploring if you have very limited or no outdoor space.

Wormery A wormery takes up very little room and is easy to make with a couple of plastic boxes with some holes drilled through for air circulation. You need to buy 'tiger worms' to get started. You can also buy a wormery as a kit, complete with worms. A wormery allows you to compost chopped-up kitchen waste and turn it into nutrient-rich vermicompost.

TIPS FOR A PRODUCTIVE COMPOST PILE

- Position your compost pile in a shady spot – direct sunlight dries it out. If it is completely open, a semi-sheltered spot (such as under a tree or by a hedge) is ideal.
- It is best to have the base of the pile in contact with the soil to allow for drainage and for worms and microbes to pass up into the pile.
- If you must build your compost pile on concrete, start it off with plenty of twigs to create drainage and airflow and add a bucket of soil from elsewhere in the garden to kick it off with active soil microbes.
- The larger your compost pile, the hotter the centre gets; the hotter the centre, the quicker it breaks down.
- An aerated, hot compost pile helps to reduce the risk of passing on disease from one season to the next.

Ratios As a general rule, you want one part nitrogen-rich green waste to two parts carbon-rich brown waste. I see it like a sandwich: the brown materials are the bread that holds everything together and creates structure. The green materials are the filling, which add nutrients and nitrogen to help everything break down.

Alternate layers Make a compost lasagne, adding different materials and layering no more than a few centimetres of brown or green at a time.

Aerate Oxygen is vital to a compost pile. To ensure the pile is aerobic, aim to turn it every two to three months using a spade or fork.

Water Moisture is essential for the decomposition process. If the weather has been particularly dry, water your compost pile to keep it moist and keep microbes alive and active.

What can go in? Any raw, organic materials.

GREEN WASTE IS RICH IN NITROGEN

- Grass clippings
- Fresh leaves, deadheaded flowers
- Some weeds (see note on weeds opposite)
- Kitchen waste (vegetable peelings, coffee grounds, clean eggshells)
- Manure

BROWN WASTE IS RICH IN CARBON

- Cardboard
- Tissues
- Dry leaves
- Straw
- Hedge trimmings
- Small twigs
- Woodchip

An active compost pile using an open bay system

bin, add them to a bucket of water for a few weeks until they rot down a bit and become a stinky slime. This denatures seeds and roots. The slimy, stinky mix can then be poured over the compost pile to add nutrients and moisture.

Got worms? A healthy compost pile will be full of worms after a few months. They munch through waste and speed up the composting process, churning and mixing things up as they eat their way through the pile. You may want to encourage worms by collecting them from other areas of the garden or buying them in from a garden centre or tackle shop.

When is it ready? Depending on the time of year, and the quality and size of the compost pile, it can take anywhere between three and 12 months to get good, usable compost. When compost is ready it will look like compost, smell like earth, and be crumbly and light. Well-made compost won't smell bad or feel slimy. If it does, you probably added too much green material. Not to worry – you can fix it by re-layering it with more brown material.

What can't go in? Cooked food, dairy, bones, meat and carnivorous animal waste, as it can entice rats and dangerous pathogens. Anything with hidden plastics (cardboard film/lining, most tea bags, sticky tape) as these won't decompose. Perennial weeds that spread by runners or that have formed seed heads, such as brambles, docks and mare's tail, as these will spread if put straight into the compost pile. Instead of chucking them in the

Grow
Discover the best food to nurture in your plot

Choosing your plants

KEY

Sun / Shade / Part shade

ANY   Soil type

Sow

Plant

Harvest

There is such a huge array of edible plants to grow, that it can become almost bewildering. To help you decide, start simple: grow things you like to eat and things you will use. Focus on crops that offer maximum production with minimal input, space and expense.

It is unlikely you will become self-sufficient in homegrown produce from back-garden growing, so why use precious space to grow staples such as baking potatoes when these are relatively cheap to buy and largely unexciting? Focus your growing efforts on super veg: hard-to-find, unusual, accent edibles such as tomatoes, sugar snap peas and chillies.

Pests and diseases

These are mentioned briefly under each entry in this chapter. For more detail and solutions to several pests and diseases, see the dedicated section from p141.

GLOSSARY

These terms come up throughout the book, so to avoid confusion this section provides simple definitions.

Bolt When a leaf or root crop produces flowers and begins the process of setting seed. This reduces and eventually halts production of the leaves, roots or shoots it was grown for. Bolting can be caused by stress, such as too little water or not enough nutrients.

Cold frame See p44.

Companion plant A plant that is beneficial to another plant growing nearby, or two plants that are mutually beneficial to each other. Examples could include one plant acting as a pest deterrent. See p17 for more information.

Cultivar This is a 'cultivated variety', which means a plant that has been produced by selective breeding.

Direct sow See p42.

Go to seed When a plant begins to make seed heads. See also: Bolt. Leafy vegetables in particular become bitter or tough once flowers develop.

Hardening off The process of acclimatising plants grown indoors to cooler temperatures outdoors by gradually taking them outdoors for periods each day.

Hardiness A plant's ability to withstand cold temperatures.

Heirloom A historic plant variety. These are essential for maintaining genetic diversity in crops. See p22.

Mulch A layer of organic matter placed on growing beds or around growing plants to suppress weeds, aid water retention, insulate roots and add nutrients. There are inorganic mulches, such as gravel. See p136 for more information.

Open pollination Flowere pollinated naturally by wind, birds or insects.

Pinch out Picking off the growing tip or side shoots above leaf nodes to encourage bushy growth.

Plant out See p43.

Potash Horticultural term for the nutrient potassium.

Pot bound When a plant outgrows the container it is in and the roots become cramped. At this point the plant will need to be potted into a new, larger container.

Pot on See p43.

Prick out To transplant (lift and move) seedlings from where they germinated into a bigger pot to continue growing.

Runner Aerial stem that comes from a mother plant as a method of proliferation – as the stem touches the ground, it has a chance to root and create a new plant.

Thinning The process of removing seedlings to leave only stronger ones or to achieve good spacing between plants. Can also refer to removing excess plant parts (e.g. thinning leaves).

True leaves See p43.

Vermiculite A very light, expanded mineral that helps with moisture retention and drainage in compost.

Leafy greens

Leafy salad greens are some of the easiest plants to grow. They shoot up fast and produce a generous harvest in a small space – even a window box will give a rewarding crop. Most salad greens deteriorate rapidly once picked, as shown by supermarket salad leaves in plastic bags, which go mushy in days. To get around that, stagger your sowing so that you sow a fresh batch every couple of weeks. This will give you a continuous and steady (rather than overwhelming) supply of fresh, crisp and nutritious leafy greens throughout the year.

Chard / *Beta vulgaris* **subsp. *cicla* var. *flavescens*** ↗ →

🌿 FEB–MAR INDOORS / MAR–SEP DIRECT

☀ ◐ (ANY) H: 5–50CM 🗓 ALL YEAR

The humble but mighty chard, where would we be without it? When all other salads, spinach and leaf brassicas have been munched by slugs and caterpillars, chard will have your back. I love chard because it grows just about anywhere and throughout the entire growing year. What's more, it comes in a joyful array of colours (such as this ruby chard, pictured) that brighten any garden and dish.

STARTING OFF Sow in individual modules in early spring or direct at almost any time of year when the ground isn't frozen or very cold. Chard will come up when it's ready. If you want to pick baby leaves, sow thickly and directly around 2–5cm apart. For larger, full-sized chard, aim to have the final spacing at 10–20cm. I like to sow thickly to begin with and pull full plants out when young to use in salads, leaving behind well-spaced plants to grow to full size for year-round use.

GROWING ON Chard requires regular watering in warm weather to stop it from going to seed, but needs little else.

PESTS AND DISEASES For a leafy green, chard is reasonably bullet-proof in terms of pests, though it can be nibbled by slugs when young and is prone to the occasional pigeon attack. If pigeons are a problem, try netting or building a cage around plants with small branches. Beet leaf miner can also cause damage. The main disease to look out for is cercospora leaf spot, which causes small, reddish-brown, round blotches on the leaves, weakening the plant. There is no homemade cure for this: simply cut away infected leaves to control the disease.

HARVEST Pick baby leaf chard when under 10cm for salads. Pick bigger leaves at any point for cooking.

Corn salad / *Valerianella locusta* ↗

🌱 MAR–MAY OR SEP–OCT DIRECT ☀ ◐

(MOST) H: UP TO 20CM 🧺 ALL YEAR

Corn salad (also known as lamb's lettuce) may be my favourite leaf

crop of all time, producing mini rosettes of deep green leaves with a nutty, savoury flavour. Its virtues are endless: it's bulletproof in terms of pests and disease and requires little protection against slugs or birds. It also grows pretty much anywhere, in shade or sun. It stays mild, tender and sweet even after frosts, preferring cooler temperatures and damp weather. It will happily self-sow if left to flower. Try interplanting it with larger crops in summer.

STARTING OFF Sow directly in the ground in spring or early autumn, aiming for seeds to be 3–5cm apart. Cover lightly with soil and keep well watered.

GROWING ON Corn salad needs regular watering to keep it from bolting, especially in warm weather.

Top 'Red Oak Leaf' **Bottom** 'Winter Marvel'

PESTS AND DISEASES Slugs can attack tiny seedlings, but as they mature the plants hold their own and generally do not need protection.

HARVEST Pick individual leaves or pull whole rosettes as needed (see p151).

← ↙ Lettuce / *Lactuca sativa*

🌱 MAR–MAY INDOORS / APR–AUG DIRECT

☀ ◑ (ANY) H: 5–50CM 🧺 APR–NOV

Lettuce can be so much more exciting than the plain old iceberg you find at the supermarket. When you grow your own you can experiment with less common varieties such as 'Red Oak Leaf', 'Speckled Butterhead' and beautiful 'Little Red Gems'. Lettuce is easy to grow and fast growing, and it works well as an interplanting crop when grown between tall brassicas.

STARTING OFF You can start off spring sowings indoors. Sow one seed per module at a depth of 1cm. This gives young plants protection from predators and will allow individual plants to make healthy root systems that can be transplanted outside with minimum root disturbance. You can also sow direct into a prepared growing bed or in a window box or large, shallow pot. For cut-and-come again lettuces, aim for seeds to be spaced 2–3cm apart. For full-sized lettuce heads, sow seeds around 5–6cm apart and then thin them further (eating the thinned seedlings as your first crop), aiming for a final spacing of 15–20cm.

GROWING ON Lettuce should be kept well watered in dry spells to prevent bolting.

PESTS AND DISEASES Early sown lettuce can be prone to pigeon attack so protect them with twiggy branches or netting. Check around the edges of pots and beds for slugs and snails, particularly after rain and consider using a barrier method such as wool pellets (see p147) as lettuce is one of their favourite foods.

HARVEST Lettuce can be harvested at any point during its growing period. See p151 for cut-and-come-again varieties.

Malabar spinach / *Basella alba*

APR–MAY INDOORS ☀ RICH
H: UP TO 5M 🧺 SUMMER

Botanically speaking, malabar spinach is not a true spinach, though it is used in cooking in much the same way. It is a climbing plant that sends out sprawling shoots and can become monstrous in size. It is a stunning plant available in green- and red-stemmed varieties that put on a glistening show in full sun. Its shiny, almost succulent leaves are delicious both raw and cooked and have a slightly peppery, citrus flavour.

STARTING OFF Start malabar spinach off from seed indoors or in a heated propagator in mid-spring. The seedlings are chunky and fast growing, so sow into individual pots.

It can also be started off from cuttings taken from side shoots.

GROWING ON Plant out when danger of frost has passed. Provide a trellis or growing support for the vines. Originating from tropical regions, it does best in warm, wet weather. If allowed to dry out in the heat, it may send out flowers: once in flower the leaves become a little bitter and tough so keep well watered. It is not frost tolerant, so in autumn, before the ground freezes, cut back the leaves, pot up the roots and bring the plant inside. You can plant it back out in spring when the last frost has passed.

PESTS AND DISEASES Malabar spinach grows so big that pests aren't usually too much of a problem. Even if slugs and snails have a nibble there is still plenty to harvest. Young plants need protection though. It is prone to cercospora leaf spot: cut off any leaves that have red-brown spots on them to keep this fungal infection at bay.

HARVEST Unlike regular spinach (which does not do well in hot weather), malabar spinach has its peak in summer, so can bridge the gap in between spinach harvests. If the vines are becoming unruly, snip entire stems for use, or just take a few leaves at a time, leaving plenty on the plant to photosynthesise.

Rocket / *Eruca vesicaria*
subsp. *sativa* ↑

🌱 MAR–SEP DIRECT ☀ ◑
(ANY) H: 5–60CM 🧺 MAR–NOV

Salad rocket is grown as an annual and has bigger and fleshier leaves than its cousin, wild rocket (*Diplotaxis tenuifolia*), which is a perennial plant. Wild rocket is much stronger in flavour, slower growing and much hardier, often producing harvests deep into winter. Salad rocket does well in full sun early in spring and in autumn, but will bolt in hot, dry weather, so it is best to interplant between taller plants when sowing in the summer months, to give it some shade.

STARTING OFF Sow seeds direct where they are to grow in beds or large pots. Sow thickly, 0.5–1cm deep, aiming for a spacing of around 1–2cm.

GROWING ON Rocket likes a sunny spot but will grow pretty much in any position in any soil.

PESTS AND DISEASES Young rocket seedlings can be nibbled by slugs. Rocket is in the *Brassicaceae* family, so is also prone to flea beetle.

HARVEST Rocket can be harvested using the cut-and-come again method (see p151). Snip the leaves once they are 10–15cm tall (leave the centre intact to about 2cm tall to grow on). Alternatively, pick thickly sown rocket carefully, plucking individual plants from the ground, leaving a final spacing of 10cm between each plant so that they can grow on to full size.

Sorrel / *Rumex* spp.

🌱 MAR–MAY DIRECT ☀ ◑
(RICH) H: UP TO 1M 🧺 MAR–NOV

The sorrel family has a distinct lemony flavour and succulent leaves. It grows pretty much like a weed and is largely unaffected by pests and disease, making it a favourite for edible gardens. Sorrel thrives in moisture-retentive soil, grows in part shade or full sun, and is perfect for damp, semi-shaded corners of the garden. This perennial will die back in hard frosts, reappearing in the spring.

I love French sorrel (*Rumex scutatus*), also known as buckler-leaved sorrel, with its small, arrow-shaped leaves that have an almost bluish hue. Another favourite is common sorrel

(*R. acetosa*), which has huge, bright green leaves, perfect for adding a citrusy flavour to soups. Red-vein sorrel (*R. sanguineus*) has a very attractive, bright green leaf with contrasting red veins, but in my opinion is much less tasty than the green varieties and tougher in texture.

STARTING OFF Sprinkle seeds thinly, directly in their growing spot. Cover with a little soil and water well.

GROWING ON Plant sorrel in a sheltered area, under the shade of bigger plants or in dappled shade, and keep it well watered as it can become stressed in hot, dry conditions. Cut away any flower spikes that begin to form to keep leaf production going. By doing this, sorrel can produce fresh greenery throughout the year, even in winter.

PESTS AND DISEASES Slugs and birds may have the occasional nibble but it is largely pest-hardy.

HARVEST Pick the larger, outer leaves as needed.

Winter purslane / *Claytonia perfoliata*

🌱 FEB–APR OR AUG–OCT DIRECT ☀️ ◐
(ANY) H: 5–40CM 🧺 ALL YEAR

Also known as miner's lettuce, this is a 'weed' that I actively encourage in my veg patches. It is so high in vitamins A and C that it was eaten by miners during the American gold rush in the mid-nineteenth century to prevent scurvy. It creates beautiful basal rosettes of long-stemmed, teardrop-shaped leaves that are juicy and sweet for most of the cooler months of the year, providing a valuable salad crop throughout winter. It likes full winter sun, but struggles in the midsummer sun and may die off. If you allow it to go to flower, it will set seed and pop up again when conditions are right. It also grows beautifully in light shade and does well planted in the partial shade between squashes and brassicas.

STARTING OFF Sprinkle the seeds thickly and directly in their growing spot, cover with a fine layer of soil and water well.

GROWING ON Keep well watered, especially in warmer weather. If winter purslane begins to flower and you have the space, allow the flowers to set seed – it will begin popping up everywhere, becoming the most welcome weed.

PESTS AND DISEASES Not many critters bother it. Very young plants can be the subject of slug attacks and hungry birds may have a nibble.

HARVEST Harvest when leaves are over 7cm in length, cutting the outer leaves as needed and leaving the inner heart (the rosette of leaves) intact; this way you will get a cut-and-come-again salad leaf (see p151). Alternatively, pull up entire plants, cutting away the tiny roots before use.

Gourmet weeds

Weeds are resilient plants that find a way to grow just about anywhere – so they will pop up in your veg patch, guaranteed. Some, such as brambles, bindweed and dock, can be a pain to eradicate and the process can take years. Others I welcome in the garden and even let self-sow. Allowing weeds to grow requires no fuss or extra work and can provide a crop when others fail. Some annual weeds provide great ground cover under and around crops to reduce moisture loss, encourage beneficial pollinators and even fix nitrogen. Many weeds can become allies – delicious, nutritious allies at that! So get to know the weeds in your space to work out friend from foe. My advice: get a good book or resource to help you identify all weeds correctly before eating them, because some are edible and tasty, and some are poisonous.

Alexanders / *Smyrnium perfoliatum*
Often spotted along roadsides, verges and in grasslands, this weed isn't known for popping up in the garden, but it is well worth introducing to semi-shaded areas. Some gardeners even propagate it as a cottage-garden plant owing to its beautiful, large leaves and seed heads. While it can get very large, it is easy to control if unwanted plants are pulled when young. Alexanders has been used as a food and medicine since at least Roman times. The young leaves and hollow stems are delicious steamed, while the ripe, black seed heads were once known as 'black potherb'. They lend a spicy, slightly aniseed flavour to foods. Bear in mind Alexanders is a member of the parsley (*Apiaceae*) family, which contains a number of poisonous species, so be sure to get a 100 per cent accurate identification before consuming.

Chickweed / *Stellaria media* ↓
This cute, sprawling plant has tiny, white, star-shaped flowers. The leaves

taste fresh and green and, if kept well watered, remain soft and juicy throughout the whole growing season. It drops seed and spreads readily, but has shallow roots that are easy to pull, so it can be controlled without fuss. Allow it to grow in a shady patch, perhaps under the leaves of a pumpkin plant, and add it to salads. Slugs avoid it, so even if all of your lettuce heads get eaten, chickweed will save the day.

Dandelion / *Taraxacum officinale*
Dandelions are one of the first flowers to bloom in spring, making them an excellent food source for early bugs and bees. The flowers, leaves and roots are all edible and have been used in medicine for centuries. They are high in vitamin A, zinc and potassium and the young leaves add a bitter, fresh kick to any salad. As many gardeners know, they spread easily via their fairy-like seeds. If you would like to keep them in check, simply eat all the flowers before they set seed. Or just pick the seed heads off.

Garlic mustard / *Alliaria petiolata* ↗
Also known as jack-by-the-hedge, garlic mustard is a beautiful hedgerow plant that often finds its way into gardens. The leaves taste of – you guessed it – a mix between garlic and

mustard, with a hint of bitterness that increases as the plant matures. The large, shiny, heart- or kidney-shaped leaves can be used like vine leaves and stuffed with rice or cheese, or be simply cooked like spinach.

Ground elder / *Aegopodium podagraria*
Ground elder is a rampant weed that spreads via rhizomes and grows just about anywhere. I do not suggest introducing it in your garden. But if you have it growing already it is worth noting that the young spring leaves are quite delicious, tasting fresh and green with a hint of lovage. Use them as you

would spinach, by wilting slightly and adding to soups, omelettes and pastas. Avoid eating the leaves after the plant has flowered as they become tough and bitter and can have a laxative effect. As with alexanders (see p64), this a member of the *Apiaceae* family, so be extra careful with identification before consuming.

Nettle / *Urtica dioica*

Nettles are an important food plant for many butterflies, including red admirals, commas and small tortoiseshells. They are also incredibly nutritious for humans, being high in protein, vitamins and minerals. Nettle soup in spring is simply delicious and it is worth letting a small patch grow if you have the space. Nettles spread via creeping roots and seed, so if you want to keep them in check, grow in a pot and cut back regularly so they do not drop their seeds. In fact, cutting nettles regularly ensures fresh growth of new leaves that can be harvested nearly all year round.

Plantain / *Plantago* spp. →

Lanceolate or long-leaved plantain (*Plantago lanceolata)* and broad-leaved plantain (*P. major*) are the most common varieties and often considered weeds that pop up in paths and lawns. Plantains are beautiful and green and

much hardier than standard grass varieties. I let them grow and self-sow as they keep lawns looking lush even in drought and the flowers provide food for all kinds of beneficial insects. What's more, the leaves are delicious and nutritious. They are a little tough for salads, but I like the leaves cooked as you would cook kale – steamed and added to stews. They can be tossed in oil, garlic and paprika and cooked in a low oven to crisp up as a kind of alternative kale chip. You can eat the young spring leaves raw. The flower buds of *P. lanceolata* are also edible and taste like mushrooms.

Three-cornered leek / *Allium triquetrum* →

These oniony weeds are delicious and abundant. They pop up just about anywhere and are quite rampant – so much so that they are considered invasive and must not be introduced into the wild. I strongly recommend that you do not plant them because of their invasiveness, but if you have them growing already, they are delicious and all parts can be eaten: leaves, bulbs, flowers and seed heads.

Wild garlic / *Allium ursinum*

Wild garlic (or ramson) is a plant that pops up in the early spring and fills that hungry gap before much is ready to harvest in the garden. All parts can be eaten (leaves, flowers, seed heads and bulbs). Wild garlic grows best in shady, wooded areas, making it perfect for those with low-light growing spaces.

Wood sorrel / *Oxalis* spp. →

These cute, clover-like woodland plants grow with ease in shady areas. The leaves have a tart, citrusy flavour just like cultivated sorrel (*Rumex*, see p62). They make a beautiful garnish, but should be eaten in moderation as they contain oxalic acid, which should not be consumed in quantity.

Legumes

Legumes are in the *Fabaceae* family and are varied in form and flavour, ranging from the garden pea to multicoloured beans. Not only do legumes offer us protein, they also fix nitrogen in the soil with the help of bacteria and tiny nodules in their roots. For this reason, after the plants have put out their last fruits, cut the parts above ground leaving the roots in the soil to decompose, adding nutrients as they break down.

Broad bean / *Vicia faba* →

🫘 OCT–NOV DIRECT (HARDY VARIETIES)
FEB–MAR INDOORS (HARDY VARIETIES)
MAR–APR DIRECT (TENDER VARIETIES)

☀️ (RICH) H: 50CM–1.2M 🧺 MAY–JUL

I have a love-hate relationship with broad beans. The pros are that they can be planted in winter when there is little else going on and, of course, that they're tasty, beautiful (like 'Grano Violetto', pictured) and sometimes bountiful. The cons are that they are host to myriad pests and diseases, leading to lost crops. Some gardeners have brilliant success, while others find them impossible to get a worthwhile crop from. Give them a go, though – you never know, you may be one of the lucky ones.

STARTING OFF Early winter sowings can be done direct in the soil for hardy varieties in mild areas. This usually results in an earlier crop the following spring and early summer. An indoor sowing in root trainer module trays or toilet rolls in early spring can help strengthen plants before planting out (see instructions for peas on p70). Alternatively, broad beans can be sown direct once soil temperatures have warmed a little in early to mid-spring. Sow at a depth of 3–5cm with a final spacing of 15–20cm.

GROWING ON Tall cultivars may require staking but many are self-supporting. Like all legumes, broad beans love lots of sun, water and nutrients. When the lowest truss of flowers has formed, pinch out the growing tip to encourage fruiting. The tips can be eaten.

PESTS AND DISEASES Young plants are subject to slug and bird attack. As pods begin to develop, rodents such as rats and squirrels can become a problem. Broad beans are susceptible to a fungal infection called chocolate spot – prune leaves as soon as you spot it to stop it spreading. Aphids also love them.

HARVEST Broad beans can be harvested while pods are small (6–8cm) and eaten whole. For shelling beans, younger beans are sweeter: pick pods when the beans begin to become visible through the pods but before they become overly mature. The scar – the small 'lip' on each bean – should still be green. When this scar turns black, they can become bitter.

French bean / *Phaseolus vulgaris* ↗
🫘 APR–JUL INDOORS ☀️ (RICH)
H: 1–4M 🧺 JUL–SEP

Compared with peas and broad beans, French beans are as easy to grow in containers as they are in the ground. They come in climbing or dwarf varieties. Dwarf beans crop quickly and are self-supporting, but only fruit for a few weeks, so repeat sowings are needed for continual harvests.

Climbing varieties require tall, sturdy bean poles to grow up and take longer to fruit, but do so over a long period of time. As they grow vertically, climbing beans produce a large crop in relatively little ground space.

STARTING OFF French beans like warmth to germinate, so start them off indoors in mid- to late spring in root trainer modules or empty toilet rolls (see instructions for peas on p70). Sow one seed per module or roll at a depth of 2–3cm. When plants reach 10cm in height they can be planted out. They benefit from hardening off and can be planted out in late spring or early summer once all danger of frost has passed. Plant in containers or in the ground at a spacing of 10–15cm. Use strong bamboo, willow or hazel canes for support as they grow. Add short twiggy sticks between rows to give baby plants something to grab on to until they are big enough to wrap around the canes.

GROWING ON French beans like lots of sun, water and rich soil. They benefit from a compost mulch just as the flower buds begin to form.

PESTS AND DISEASES Bean seedlings are prime tucker for slugs, snails, mice and birds. Protect them while they are young. Aphids can also be a problem.

HARVEST Pick beans regularly to extend their harvesting period. Pods are best picked young, when under 15cm in length and before the beans inside begin to mature.

Pea / *Pisum sativum* →

🌢 FEB–MAR INDOORS / APR–JUN DIRECT

☀️ (RICH) H: 50CM–2.5M 🧺 JUN–OCT

If you haven't grown your own peas yet, I urge you to give it a go. Supermarket peas don't come close to a fresh pea from the garden. Eat them as soon as possible after picking as the sweetness converts from sugars to starches quickly once they are off

the plant. The easiest and quickest varieties to grow are mangetout (like 'Golden Sweet', pictured) and sugar snap, which are eaten pod and all. Garden peas require a little more time and attention as they are picked when pods are more mature. Peas are generally split into three categories: first earlies, second earlies and maincrop. If you have the space, choose multiple types so you can harvest them in succession throughout the growing season.

STARTING OFF Peas can germinate in cooler temperatures (as low as 4ºC) but prefer it warmer, so start them under cover or direct sow from mid-spring. The tender seedlings are prone to slug attack so I find it better to start them inside in modules anyway. They have long root systems that do not like to be disturbed, so rather than a propagation tray, use a root trainer module (these can be bought online) or toilet paper tubes.

To sow peas in toilet rolls, place empty rolls in a propagation tray and fill with compost (pictured on p42). Sow one seed per roll. The benefit of planting them in cardboard rolls is they can be planted, roll and all, with minimal disturbance to the roots. Sow peas at a depth of 1–2cm. Once the seedlings are about 10cm high, they are ready to plant out at a spacing of around 10–15cm. I like to plant mine in a zig-zag formation to maximise space and create an extra row.

GROWING ON Most pea varieties need support in the form of canes and string or pea netting. I try to keep my use of plastic in the garden to a minimum, and I usually find pea netting ends up a tangled mess and small birds can get trapped in it. So instead I use pea sticks: small twiggy branches that the plants can clamber up (this looks prettier too). Some peas can reach heights of up to 2.5m, while dwarf cultivars require minimal support. Check the height of your pea before planting out so you can build a suitable climbing structure (see p47).

Peas are thirsty, hungry plants, especially as they begin to flower. When the first buds appear, add a 2–5cm layer of compost mulch around their roots to prevent moisture loss and encourage plentiful flowering. Water regularly at this point and throughout fruiting to ensure a good harvest.

PESTS AND DISEASES Young, pea seedlings are targeted by slugs, snails, birds and mice. Starting them off inside helps to toughen them up a bit, but take precautions until plants are at least 30cm high and try sowing around 20 per cent more than you need to make up for losses. Powdery mildew tends to affect plants as they mature and come to the end of production. Pea moth can also damage a crop.

HARVEST Pick sugar snaps just as the pods fill. Pick mangetout while the pods are still flat and tender. And harvest garden peas once the pods are full but before they get too mature and lose their sweetness. They are so tasty it's unlikely many will make it to the kitchen before being munched straight from the plant.

Runner bean / *Phaseolus coccineus* →

APR INDOORS / MAY–JUN DIRECT   ☀   (RICH)
H: 1M–4M   🧺   JUL–OCT

Runner beans are productive and easy to grow. While dwarf varieties are available, most runner beans are climbing plants, clambering vertically up whatever support they are given, producing copious pods of beans as they go.

STARTING OFF Sow runner bean seeds at a depth of around 3–4cm indoors in large module trays or individual 9cm pots from mid-spring or direct in their growing spot from late spring to early summer. The final spacing for runner beans is around 15cm apart.

GROWING ON Runner beans do not tolerate cold well, so do not plant out until all danger of frost has passed – ideally when both day and nighttime temperatures are above 12°C. They like enriched soil, so dig in plenty of compost to their final growing spot before sowing or planting out.

Build tall supports, using at least 2m-long poles of hazel, bamboo or willow. Get creative with building these: they are a thing of beauty in

or two plants to give them adequate space to grow.

PESTS AND DISEASES Slugs and snails need to be kept in check when plants are young; once above 50cm or so high, they are usually big enough to look after themselves. Aphids tend to become a problem for runner beans. In wet conditions, plants can be prone to fungal infections: cut away any diseased leaves as soon as you notice them to avoid contagion. In dry, warm conditions spider mite can also be a problem.

HARVEST Runner beans are ready to harvest from around midsummer. Pick pods while young and tender at around 15–20cm in length before they develop tough strings. Pick pods regularly, checking them every few days as frequent picking keeps the plants producing.

the veg patch. Try an A-frame support by pushing two pairs of long poles into the ground. Lean each pair against each other to create an X-shape and secure with string. Add a central pole laid across the top. Secure this with string too.

If growing in pots or if space is restricted, try a teepee shape by creating a circle of poles pushed into the ground and tied together at the top (see p50). Runner beans like a fair amount of space as their leaves grow quite large, so allow one pole per one

Microgreens

Despite their tiny stature, microgreens are packed full of flavour and nutrition and offer leaves even in the depths of winter when little else is growing. They add beautiful colour and texture to dishes and can be used as a fancy garnish or in bulk as a salad base.

Microgreens are essentially the seedlings of leafy herbs and plants that are sown thickly and harvested when very young. They can be grown quickly: you can get a crop in as little as seven days. If sown in succession, sowing a fresh batch every couple of weeks, you'll have a continuous supply, year-round.

There are a few edibles I prefer to grow as microgreens, rather than full-sized crops. Coriander, for instance, often bolts as it gets older and produces tougher leaves and stems as it goes to flower, so I tend to sow it thickly and harvest the smaller leaves.

Growing microgreens costs next to nothing. All you need is a shallow tray – recycled punnets from strawberries and mushrooms are handy vessels – and a thin layer of compost. You can source seeds from the supermarket by using whole spices such as coriander, mustard and fennel seeds. Other seeds available at low cost from supermarkets include sunflower seeds and dried peas. Radish, broccoli or kale microgreens

can be grown from your own saved seed if you allow your crops to flower. Here are some of my favourites.

Alfalfa	Coriander	Mustard
Basil	Fennel	Radish
Beetroot	Kale	Rocket
Broccoli	Lettuce	Spinach
Chard	Mizuna	Sweetcorn

Method Place a 2–3cm layer of fine/sieved compost in a tray and sprinkle over your seed of choice thickly, aiming for a distance of anywhere between a few millimetres to 1cm between seeds (experiment with different distances for different varieties to get the spacing right). Cover with a fine layer of vermiculite and sprinkle with water. If you don't have any vermiculite, leave your seeds on the surface of the soil and keep damp by spraying with water a few times a day.

Microgreens can also be grown without soil, using felt or a few layers of dampened kitchen roll placed in a seed tray, though this method can cause seeds to dry out quickly, so they'll need more attention and watering.

Apart from sweetcorn (which needs at least 14ºC), most of the microgreen seeds listed on the opposite page will germinate in cool temperatures, but in very cold weather (below 8ºC) start them off on a windowsill for best results.

Solanaceae family

The nightshade (*Solanaceae*) family includes many familiar edibles such as tomatoes, peppers, aubergines and potatoes. This section covers those that fruit above ground – you'll find more information about potatoes in the root vegetable section on p95.

Aubergine / *Solanum melongena* →

🌱 FEB–MAR INDOORS ☀ (RICH)
H: 40CM–1M 🧺 JUL–NOV

Aubergines grow as perennials in the tropical climates of Africa and South Asia from where they originate, but behave as half-hardy annuals in temperate climates. To do well in northern Europe, they require a long growing season and plenty of sun and warmth to set fruit. They fruit best when grown in a greenhouse, polytunnel or on a sunny windowsill but can be grown outside in a sheltered spot or close to a sunny wall, which helps retain and radiate heat. There is a huge range of aubergine varieties out there, coming in many different colours and shapes, from long and white to fat and purple striped. I always pick varieties that are early maturing, such as 'Czech Early' (pictured), but my favourite in terms of productivity and taste is plain old 'Black Beauty'.

Opposite A crop of 'Primabella' cherry tomatoes in early September

STARTING OFF Sow seeds at a depth of 0.5–1cm in modules or small pots in February and keep them warm, either in a heated propagator or on a sunny windowsill.

GROWING ON Prick out seedlings when they develop true seed leaves and transplant to 9cm pots. When the roots begin to fill the pots, transfer to 30cm pots or larger and grow on inside or plant straight into a sheltered, sunny spot outdoors or in a prepared bed in a polytunnel. Pinch out plants when they reach 30cm tall to encourage bushier growth. Feed with a high-potassium liquid fertiliser every two weeks once flowers and fruits appear.

PESTS AND DISEASES Aubergines are very prone to spider mite. To help prevent this, keep leaves moist by misting them regularly (see p148 for more on spider mite control). Aphids can also be a problem. Keep your plants, especially those grown in pots, well watered and mulched to avoid blossom-end rot on fruits.

HARVEST Harvest when fruits reach the mature colour intended for that variety. For most aubergines the general rule is to pick when they are fat and juicy and before they lose their shine.

Pepper / *Capsicum* spp. →

FEB–MAR INDOORS

RICH   H: 40CM–1M   JUL–NOV

Glossy, colourful and diverse, peppers come in so many shapes, sizes and flavours aside from the usual bell variety. They make attractive pot plants that thrive on sunny windowsills, or in a greenhouse or conservatory. For sweet peppers, choose heritage varieties that have been bred to ripen in the cooler, northern parts of the world. I love 'Chocolate Bell', 'Sweet Yellow Stuffing Pepper' and 'Orange Horizon', all of which are early cropping varieties.

While peppers aren't a natural choice for outdoor growing in the UK, they can do well in warmer summers. If space is limited and you can only grow one windowsill pepper, it may be worth choosing a chilli pepper as they go a lot further in dishes. 'Black Fang' is especially beautiful, but does grow tall and wide. 'Kashmiri' (pictured) is great for drying. 'Lemon Drop' is a mild, citrus-flavoured yellow chilli that adds a real depth of flavour to foods. If space is really limited, try 'Pretty In Purple', which grows into a compact bush and forms short, fat fruits that are multicoloured at different stages of maturity, ranging from green to red and eventually deep purple. They look beautiful as a houseplant and are mega hot – guaranteed to please chilli heads.

STARTING OFF Pepper seeds require constant warmth of around 16–21ºC to germinate, so for best results start them off on a sunny windowsill or heated propagator, one or two seeds per small pot or module. They need a long growing season to ripen and produce fruit, so plant early in February if possible.

GROWING ON Prick out seedlings as they grow true leaves and pot them on into 9cm containers. For bushier plants, pinch out the growing tips when they reach about 20cm and then pot on to even larger pots, 30cm or more if you have the space. As flowers begin to appear, add a fresh compost or soil and liquid feed weekly. If the soil in your pepper pots becomes too dry or the roots are exposed, apply 3–5cm of mulch (such as well-rotted manure or compost). Plants may need staking or caging as fruits develop.

PESTS AND DISEASES Protect young plants from slugs and snails and watch out for aphids and spider mites.

HARVEST The time to harvest peppers depends on what kind of pepper you have grown. Although most seed packets say peppers mature in 60–90 days, in my experience peppers take 100–150 days to mature.

Tomato / *Solanum lycopersicum* →

🌱 JAN–EARLY APR INDOORS

☀️ (RICH) H: 50CM–2.5M 🌿 JUN–SEP

Is there anything better than a freshly picked, homegrown tomato, warm under the sun? Sweet-tart and full-flavoured, tomatoes are often the first veg people attempt to grow, though they're not the easiest, being prone to disease and requiring plenty of food, sun, love and attention. But they're well worth your time and care, and you can grow interesting varieties you'll never find in the supermarket.

Tomatoes are generally classified into two kinds of growing pattern: indeterminate (cordon) and determinate (bush) varieties. Cordon varieties grow tall (up to 2.5m high) and continually chuck out side shoots that need to be pruned so the plant can focus its energy on producing fruits. Cordons can be trained and pruned to grow tall and narrow up a cane or string, which can save space.

Bush varieties tend to grow, well, bushier. They are great for growing in containers and their fruits are usually smaller or cherry-sized, generally fruiting earlier than cordon varieties. Larger bush varieties can grow into bewildering things, sprawling across a bed and taking up a lot of space if not supported. Their side shoots do not generally need pruning – they just do their thing, producing copious amounts of fruits as they go (though they can benefit from some pruning to provide airflow at the base). The best way to tame and support bush varieties is by placing three canes in a triangle around the plant and tying them with string at various heights to create a cage that supports the plant and hanging trusses of fruit as they form (see p47). If space is limited, try dwarf bush varieties such as 'Gartenperle' or 'Tumbling Tom', which are perfect for pots and even hanging baskets.

STARTING OFF Tomatoes require a long growing season to produce fruit, so start them off indoors as early as possible. If you have a sunny windowsill, conservatory or heated greenhouse, this can be as early as January or February. Tomato seedlings need to get direct sunlight so that they grow big and bushy and do not shoot up long and leggy in search of light. I live in a very shady spot, surrounded by trees, so I have invested in a heated propagator and some grow lights – nothing fancy, just some basic, low-energy LED lights

Clockwise from top left 'Primabella', 'Garden Peach', 'Gardener's Delight' and 'Artisan Pink'

for houseplants – and they work a treat. If you do not have access to the above, start tomatoes off in a greenhouse or cold frame outside in March or April.

Sow tomato seeds in module trays of fine seed compost. They germinate best at continuous temperatures of 15°C and above. It's time to pot on when the seedlings are at a height of around 5cm and have formed true leaves. Prick them out and pot up into larger 9cm containers to allow them room to grow before planting in their final growing spot after all chance of frost has passed.

Tomatoes can grow roots from their stems (called root initials), so if your seedlings get a little leggy, you can repot them slightly deeper by burying the stem 1–3cm under the soil – this will encourage them to grow more roots and shorten the stem. Just ensure you never bury the leaves as this can cause the plant to rot.

GROWING ON Harden off tomatoes sown inside. Do this towards late spring, once the day and nighttime temperatures have been above 10°C or so for a few weeks, by taking them outside in the day and bringing them in at night to expose them to the elements a little. Then plant out in their final position, either in large pots, grow bags or in the ground, but only once all chance of frost has passed. Feed once every two to three weeks while they are seedlings. Once they start to develop flowers, feed once a week.

Tomatoes love to grow indoors in a sunny spot, in a polytunnel or greenhouse. If you have the luxury of indoor growing space, your tomatoes will thank you, producing more fruits and being less prone to disease. But don't fret, they will still produce well outside in a sunny spot.

PESTS AND DISEASES Blight. A word associated with devastation. That is no exaggeration: under the right weather conditions, you can lose your entire tomato crop to blight. For me it is usually not a case of *if* I will get blight, but *when*. I truly cannot remember a year when it has not affected my toms.

Blight is a fungal disease, spread by airborne spores that settle and reproduce in soil. It tends to set in towards the end of summer, just as your tomatoes are producing lush, green trusses of fruit. It causes black spots on leaves, stems and fruits, making tomatoes themselves black, mushy and inedible.

Winning the battle against blight is all about careful observation, control and making the conditions unfavourable for it to take hold in the first place, or at least set in later in the season when you already have a good crop of tomatoes. Blight likes warmth and humidity, so provide good spacing between tomato plants, do not allow leaves to touch the soil, remove lower leaves and keep them well pruned to allow good airflow and lessen chances of blight lingering. Water direct to the roots and avoid getting leaves wet (this is much easier with indoor-grown plants). Inspect your plants daily, removing any diseased leaves or any part of the plant with black spots – be ruthless, even if it means cutting the main stem or removing entire plants to prevent disease spreading. If you do get blight on the leaves but have good-sized, unripe tomatoes, cut off all of the leaves and leave the fruits on the stems to ripen. If blight has infected the main stem, pick the green fruits and place in a paper bag with a banana to ripen. If that fails, green tomato chutney it is!

HARVEST Harvest tomatoes one at a time as they ripen on the plant from midsummer onwards.

SAVING YOUR OWN SEED If you've grown a particularly tasty or successful tomato and you'd like to grow it again next year, try saving your own seed – though do check it's open pollinated first (see p22). It's incredibly easy and you'll end up with so many tomato seeds that you can share them with friends.

- Slice fruits in half or in quarters and squash the seeds out into a small glass or jar.
- Leave the seeds with their pulp to sit at room temperature for three days.
- Pour the gloop into a small sieve, run it under the tap, moving it about to help the jelly coating wash away.
- Lay your clean seeds on some greaseproof paper or a plate to fully dry. Once dry, store in an airtight jar.

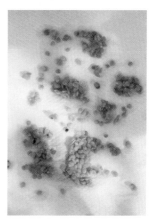

Cucurbitaceae family

The gourd family consists of nearly 100 species that include many familiar fruits and vegetables such as cucumbers, squash and melons. These are sun-loving, warm-weather, annual crops that are usually vining.

Cucumber / *Cucumis sativus* →

🌰 MAR–MAY INDOORS ☀ (RICH)
H: UP TO AROUND 2M 🧺 JUN–NOV

Cucumbers come in a wide array of colours and flavours, very different from the standard, smooth, straight, green cucumbers available in supermarkets. When growing your own, try experimenting with varieties. I particularly like tiny, bumpy cornichons, 'Moneymaker' (pictured) and 'Crystal Lemon', as well as Indian cucumbers known as kheera, which can look more like melons.

STARTING OFF Sow cucumber seeds flat (not pointy end down). Push them in around 2cm deep in individual 9cm pots. Keep seedlings warm in a greenhouse, in a heated propagator or on a sunny windowsill.

GROWING ON Cucumbers are best grown in a greenhouse or polytunnel. Though there are many outdoor varieties on the market, I always find they produce much better under cover. They are heavy

Opposite Winter squash 'Burgess Buttercup'

feeders and require lots of compost to thrive. They can be grown in large pots or planters and need a support frame (see p47) as they grow and climb fast.

PESTS AND DISEASES Young cucumber plants are prone to slug attack. As they age, the plants nearly always develop powdery mildew. While this doesn't usually kill them, it weakens them and slows down fruit production. Cut affected leaves away as soon as you see them to prevent its spread. Cucumber mosaic virus can also be an issue.

HARVEST Pick cucumbers regularly to encourage more fruiting. Harvest them before they get too large as they can become spongy and bitter.

85

Squash / *Cucurbita* spp. →

🌱 APR–MAY INDOORS, MAY–JUN DIRECT

☀️ (RICH) H: 1M OR MORE 🧺 JUN–NOV

The term squash refers to plants of the *Cucurbita* genus and includes *C. maxima*, *C. pepo* and *C. moschata*. Varieties of *Cucurbita* are categorised as either summer or winter squash.

Summer squashes include patty pans and crookneck squashes, which are generally harvested when the fruits are immature. Courgettes such as the super-tasty and dense-fleshed 'Striato di Napoli' or 'Burpee's Golden' (pictured bottom) also fall under the summer squash category, but are rarely referred to as squash as they're used so differently in the kitchen. If space is limited and you would like to train a trailing summer squash to grow vertically, try 'Tromboncino', a climbing variety that produces long, curled summer squashes that can be eaten like a courgette when young or like a squash when more mature.

Winter squash is harvested later in the season when fully mature; the seeds inside are ripe and the fruit skins have hardened. They store for much longer periods than summer squash, sometimes for months. I love the varieties 'Queensland Blue', which has an excellent flavour and storage life, and 'Ute', which is an ancient variety, developed by the Ute people of the area, now known as Colorado in the USA. It is a large, grey-green pumpkin with dense and flavoursome flesh, one of the tastiest large pumpkins out there.

Squash are very hungry plants, requiring plenty of water and nutritious soil full of well-rotted manure or compost. They always benefit from liquid feed. They aren't

a heated propagator or on a sunny windowsill. Squash seeds can be sown direct in the soil in late May or when soil temperatures have warmed. However, they are a favourite snack for slugs, so to avoid disappointment I advise starting them off a few weeks earlier indoors.

GROWING ON Plant out squash in their final growing position in late spring, after the chance of frost has passed. Squash like plenty of room and grow best in the ground, but can do well in large pots or grow bags. Prepare the growing spot for squash by digging in plenty of nutritious compost or manure. Water well throughout the growing season and they will be happy. Squash plants produce their male and female flowers on the same plant and are insect pollinated.

PESTS AND DISEASES See the list of pests and diseases for cucumber on p85.

HARVEST Harvest courgettes and crookneck squash while small and firm, usually when they are under 30cm and the skins are still soft. Pick patty pan and small summer squash when around the size of your hand (depending on the variety) and leave winter squash and pumpkins on the vine until the end of autumn, when the leaves have died back and the skins have hardened (providing the weather isn't too wet or frosty).

the most compact of things to grow, so if space is limited this may not be the crop for you. If you have a small space and have to choose just one kind of squash, go for courgettes, particularly bush varieties, as they are extremely productive and just one or two plants in the height of summer will produce more than enough courgettes to feed a family. Another space-saving option is to choose a climbing variety and train it to climb up a tree, willow structure or trellis.

STARTING OFF Sow squash seeds flat (not pointy end down) around 2cm deep in individual 9cm pots, as they get big fast. The seed leaves are some of the biggest of all the vegetable plants, so a seedling quickly outgrows a smaller pot. Keep seedlings warm in a greenhouse or, even better, in

Edible flowers

Flowers are the key to a healthy and abundant garden ecosystem, attracting pollinators and in turn birds and other helpful wildlife. While there are plenty to choose from, I like to grow flowers that are multipurpose: beautiful, fragrant, low maintenance, self-sowing and, most importantly, edible! Here are some plants that have excellent edible flowers that can be added to dishes of all kinds. Many of them also offer their own fruits, tasty leaves and even seeds. Of course, not all flowers are edible – be sure you know exactly what you're harvesting before you consume it and also be sure the flowers have been grown organically and haven't been sprayed with pesticides. Generally the petals are the best bits of a flower for eating – the centres and sepals (the green part at the base of a flower) can be bitter and are best avoided. This section refers to the edibility of the flowers for each species – unless otherwise mentioned, do not consume the rest of the plant.

Aquilegia / *Aquilegia* spp.
Also known as granny's bonnet, this beautiful, complex flower is typically purple but comes in a range of colours. It is in the buttercup (*Ranunculaceae*) family, which contains mild toxins – only the flowers are edible in moderation. After flowering, they set seed and pop up year after year.

Borage / *Borago officinalis* ↓
Borage is an old remedy said to dispel melancholy – 'borage for courage', the saying goes. Its cheery blue flowers are enough to make anyone smile. The petals taste like cucumber and can be very sweet on a sunny day. Borage is subject to slug attack when young, so plant plenty and at least a few will make it to maturity. Once fully grown, the spiky leaves are not so appealing to slugs and snails and it is pretty self-sufficient.

Brassica / *Brassicaceae*

The cabbage family includes flowering broccoli, kale, radish and more. We are all familiar with broccoli, which is bundles of unopened flower buds, but all brassicas make flowers if allowed to grow long enough. Even leafy ones such as cabbage and kale. Occasionally radish bolts too, making a flower head rather than a root. If this happens, you can pull it out, or you can let it grow on to form beautiful, cross-shaped flowers, and eat their blooms instead. The flowers of brassicas are small but numerous and attract plenty of beneficial pollinators to the garden.

Calendula / *Calendula officinalis* ↗

Also known as pot marigold, but not to be confused with marigolds (*Tagetes* spp.). In the warmer climes of its native Spain, calendula can flower at all months of the calendar year, giving rise to its name. The petals of calendula are golden orange, slightly bitter and silky on the tongue. Calendula also makes a great companion plant, luring aphids away from beans and attracting beneficial insects such as lacewings, ladybirds and hoverflies.

Campanula / *Campanula rapunculoides* **and** *C. poscharskyana*

One of the common names for this plant is bellflower – *campana* means 'bell' in Latin, which refers to its beautiful, bell-shaped, blue/purple blooms. The flowers do not have much in the way of flavour, but add plenty of beauty to food and drinks as a garnish.

Chive / *Allium schoenoprasum*

Chives begin to flower from mid-spring, forming gorgeous, purple or white buds that open into disco ball-shaped blooms. The flower buds are excellent pickled in sweet vinegar and the flowers are great sprinkled on potato salad as they lend a light, oniony flavour. Chives are robust and grow just about anywhere as long as they have plenty of sunshine. They are prone to rust disease: if they become infected, cut all parts down to the ground and allow them to regrow afresh.

Chicory / *Cichorium intybus* ↓
All parts of this tall, elegant plant are edible, though the leaves and roots are quite bitter. The roasted root is used to make a drink that tastes somewhat like coffee. The blue flowers quickly lose their colour when dry, so use them fresh in salads and drinks.

Cornflower / *Centaurea cyanus*
This wildflower was once considered a weed in corn and grain fields, giving rise to its common name. The unusual-shaped petals are bright blue and have a mild, sweet clove flavour.

Courgette / *Cucurbita pepo*
Courgette flowers are an Italian delicacy that have become popular pretty much everywhere. Courgettes send out male flowers before their female flowers to attract pollinators. Be sure to pick only a few male flowers (those borne on a stalk, rather than those with an immature fruit at their base) or you won't have any courgettes to harvest. The flowers are large and yellow and can be stuffed with rice and cheese for a delicious treat.

Evening primrose / *Oenothera biennis* ↗
Evening primrose is best known for its oil, which is extracted from its seeds and sold as a health supplement. But the petals of its bright yellow flowers are also edible. It blooms from the end of spring to the end of summer and its flowers tend to open in the late afternoon or evening. It has a lemony scent and helps to attract all kinds of flying insects.

← **Fennel /** *Foeniculum vulgare*

All aerial parts of fennel are edible but the tiny yellow flowers are especially delicious. They have a sweet, anise flavour with a touch of citrus. Wild fennel drops seed readily so you can have a constant supply year on year if you let it set seed.

Fuchsia / *Fuchsia* **spp.**

The two-tone, pendent blooms of fuchsia are one of the most striking flowers for garnishes. Their bright magenta and pink petals hold together well when the calyx (green base) is removed. They really stand out when used as cake decorations. Fuchsia grows and flowers well in part shade and requires little more than a light mulch once a year and a good pruning after flowering. You can even buy the cultivar 'FuchsiaBerry' – a variety grown for its purple, edible berries.

← **Hollyhock /** *Alcea* **spp.**

The tall and striking hollyhock is the ultimate cottage-garden flower. It puts on a showy display of trumpet-shaped flowers that come in a wide array of colours, most commonly pinks and purples. The hollyhock is related to mallows and has equally silky, tasty petals. Hollyhock is considered a short-lived perennial but is most commonly grown as a biennial. Sow it from seed every year to get a constant supply of blooms. It is best started in pots as it is prone to slug attack when young. Hollyhocks are commonly affected by rust, which usually sets in during summer and little can be done to cure it. Cut off any infected leaves to slow its progress and allow the flowers to bloom for as long as they can.

Mallow / *Malva sylvestris* and *Althaea officinalis*

All parts of common mallow (*Malva sylvestris*) and marsh mallow (*Althaea officinalis*) are edible, from root to flower. The roots of marsh mallow were once used to give the sticky, mucilaginous texture to confectionery. The leaves of common and marsh mallow are technically edible but are quite tough and need to be cooked well to be palatable. The fresh, green, wheel-shaped seed heads are known as 'cheeses' and can be nibbled straight from the plant or added to salads to give a nutty flavour and texture. The flowers have a silky texture and are delicious. Mallows are also impacted by rust (see hollyhocks on p91).

Nasturtium / *Tropaeolum* spp.

Nasturtium flowers are usually bright orange and red and have a fiery flavour! They taste sweet and floral but with a peppery kick. Nasturtiums are usually creeping in nature, but bush varieties are available. They grow well against a trellis or wall, or as ground cover. The round leaves are edible and even spicier than the flowers. Nasturtiums are annuals but self-sow readily.

Pansy/violet / *Viola* spp.

Both cultivated, ornamental pansies and wild violets are edible. Bear in mind, though, that shop-bought plug plants are usually sprayed with pesticides. For this reason it is best to start them off from seed. The flowers come in a wide range of colours and have a fresh, sweet flavour. Violas grow well in the tiny gaps of rock gardens and make excellent ground cover in shady patches or under fruit trees.

Rose / *Rosa* spp.

Rose petals smell so good you'll want to eat them, and you can! All rose petals are edible, but, as a general rule, the stronger the scent, the better the floral flavour. I love making rose petal jam.

Clockwise from top left Marsh mallow, nasturtium, apothecary's rose and pansy

Roots

Roots are not a family per se and, botanically speaking, some familiar 'root' crops aren't technically roots at all. So this is a collection of familiar (and some less familiar) rooty things.

Beetroot / *Beta vulgaris* →

🥬 MAR–JUL DIRECT ☀️ (RICH)
H: 20–50CM 🧺 MAY–NOV

I love growing beetroots. Their deep colour and flavour add an element of delight to salads, pickles, juices and cakes. To maximise the crop, I like to sow them thickly, aiming for 5–6cm apart, pulling every other beet when young to allow the others to grow to full size. They do not do well with competition in their early growth but, after thinning around midsummer, I sow radishes and baby leaf salads such as lettuce and rocket between maturing beets to maximise space.

Without fail I always grow 'Chioggia' (pictured) – a gorgeous, pink-and-white-striped beet that has rings of concentric colour when cut – and a golden beetroot variety like 'Burpee's Golden', as well as a traditional, deep red one such as 'Cylindra'.

STARTING OFF Direct sow beetroot as soon as the ground thaws in early spring. Beetroot likes rich soil, so sow seed in fine, sieved homegrown compost at a depth of 1–2cm.

GROWING ON Keep beetroot well watered, particularly in very hot weather to avoid bolting. Apply a liquid comfrey or seaweed feed a few times throughout their growing period.

PESTS AND DISEASES Slugs like to munch on young leaves and birds can also nibble at the foliage. Beet leaf miner can be an issue too.

HARVEST The great thing about beetroot is that it can be harvested whenever you want. They can be picked in late spring and summer when golf ball-sized or left to grow to full, tennis ball-sized maturity and stored throughout winter. Smaller roots tend to be sweeter and more tender for eating raw or lightly pickled, while larger beets are great for roasting. Simply pull and twist roots out of the ground, plucking out the entire plant.

Carrot / *Daucus carota* ↘

🫘 FEB–JUL DIRECT ☀️ (SANDY, POTASH RICH)

H: 30CM 🧺 MAY–OCT

The ancestral wild carrot (from which all modern carrots are bred) is a small, whitish-brown, highly aromatic and slightly bitter taproot. The cultivated sweet, crunchy and flavoursome carrots we eat today come in a wide range of shapes and colours. There are many more exciting varieties than the standard orange supermarket type. I hardly ever grow orange carrots and tend to go for rainbow-coloured varieties such as 'Jaune Obtuse du Doubs', which is a sweet yellow carrot, or 'Purple Dragon' (pictured), an intensely purple one with 'real' carrot flavour. Short-rooted, round varieties such as 'Rondo' are early maturing and great to grow in containers. Carrots thrive in light, sandy soil. Note that stony soil may result in forked roots.

STARTING OFF Sow carrot seeds direct into their growing bed or container as they do not like their roots disturbed. Create shallow troughs (3–5cm deep) in rows (15–20cm apart). Hardwood ash from a wood burner or fire pit is great for carrots as it provides potash: dig in a few handfuls to the bed before sowing. Sprinkle in your carrot seeds, aiming for them to drop 2cm apart –

this can be tricky as the seeds are tiny. Cover with 2cm of soil and water well. Thin seedlings as they appear to a distance of 5cm apart to allow them to grow on to baby carrots.

GROWING ON Keep carrots well watered in dry weather to prevent bolting. Do not fertilise carrots with nitrogen-rich feeds as this encourages leaf growth over root growth.

PESTS AND DISEASES Carrot root fly can be a problem. Try interplanting carrots in between rows of garlic or onions.

HARVEST Pull carrots as you need them throughout summer. I like to harvest every other carrot to eat as baby roots and allow the remainder to grow to full size – that way you get a longer, bigger harvest in the same size space. Fully grown carrots harvested in late summer or autumn can be lifted and stored by removing the leaves and packing them in boxes of sand. Carrots kept this way can stay fresh for months.

Potato / *Solanum tuberosum* ↗

MAR–MAY DIRECT

☀ ◗ (RICH/MOST) H: UP TO 1.2M 🧺 JUN–OCT

Potatoes are readily available in supermarkets and relatively cheap to buy, so why grow them? For variety of course! The original potato was almost certainly not white. They come in an array of colours from orange to purple, as well as different shapes and sizes. Some of my favourites to grow are 'Pink Fir Apple' – a dense, nutty salad potato – as well as 'Violette', a deep purple, oblong spud.

Potatoes are divided into three categories, according to when you plant and harvest them. First earlies or 'new' potatoes can be harvested from June onwards, do not store well, and are best picked when you plan to eat them. Second earlies (also confusingly known as 'new' potatoes) are picked in July and August and are similar to first earlies in that they do not store well and are usually used as salad potatoes. Maincrop varieties are larger, usually used for baking, roasting and mashing, and are harvested from August to October. These store well for months.

STARTING OFF Potatoes are usually grown from 'seed potatoes': potatoes that are certified virus-free as opposed to spuds bought from the supermarket. It is good practice to 'chit' potatoes – this is the process of allowing the eyes to begin to sprout before planting them. Place the seed potatoes in an egg box in early spring in light conditions (but not in direct, hot sun) until the sprouts reach 2–3cm in length. This should only take a couple of weeks.

Potatoes can be grown in large containers or direct in the ground.

For container growing, fill your chosen vessel with around 15–20cm of rich compost, place the seed potatoes 15–20cm apart, and cover with another 15cm of compost. For growing in the ground, dig a trench 15–20cm deep, heaping the dug-out soil to one side in a ridge. Place the seed potatoes at a distance of 30cm apart in rows 50–60cm apart. Cover with 15–20cm of the dug-out soil.

GROWING ON Potatoes like to be 'earthed up', which means adding more compost or soil as the plant grows. When the stems are 20–30cm high, earth them up by covering them with compost, leaving just the tips sticking out of the top. Repeat this process two to three more times as they grow. This encourages the plants to make more tubers and stabilises the growing

stems so they don't fall over and snap. Potatoes need plenty of water to produce big, juicy tubers and prevent the formation of scab.

PESTS AND DISEASES Potato blight is a fungal infection and, like tomato blight, not much can be done once it has set in. Remove infected leaves as they appear and consider digging up your spuds early before it affects and rots the whole crop.

HARVEST Dig up potatoes in accordance with what type they are. For first and second earlies, dig up potatoes once the flowers have opened and are beginning to drop and when tubers are about the size of a fat thumb/ chicken egg (depending on their shape). For maincrop potatoes, wait until the foliage begins to turn yellow then cut this back and leave spuds in the ground for another two weeks to 'cure'. Then allow them to dry off fully by laying them out in a cool, dark place before storing.

Radish / *Raphanus sativus* →

🥄 FEB–SEP DIRECT ☀️ ◐ (RICH)

H: 10–20CM 🧺 ALL YEAR

Though they are technically a brassica, I have included radishes under 'roots' for obvious reasons. Radishes are one of the fastest, easiest things to grow, as long as you grow them under the right conditions. They do not tolerate heat and bolt in hot or dry weather. Some varieties can survive frosts, giving a tasty and colourful crop when other veggies are out of season. Mooli types and 'Black Spanish' are great winter radishes and can be harvested deep into the frosty months. I particularly love 'White Icicle', as it remains mild and juicy even when huge, as well as 'Red Head' for its classic flavour.

STARTING OFF Sow radishes in spring, late summer and early autumn, avoiding the hottest weeks of the year. Sow seeds thinly 3cm apart at a depth of 1–2cm in rows spaced around 5–10cm apart. Sow directly in their final growing spot as radishes do not like to be moved.

GROWING ON Radishes don't need much. Keep them well watered in dry periods and they will do their thing. They reach maturity in around four to eight weeks, so make a sowing every few weeks for a constant supply.

PESTS AND DISEASES Slugs love radishes, as do birds, particularly when the plants are young. Flea beetles can also wreak havoc, nibbling holes in the leaves and roots of entire beds.

HARVEST To get maximum harvests in minimal space, thin seedlings to around 3cm apart while they are very small and nothing but leaf. The thinned seedlings can be eaten as microgreens (see p74). Leave the remaining radishes to grow on a little and then harvest every other radish when they are the size of hazelnuts. Leave the rest to grow to full-sized radishes and harvest before they become woody.

Alliums

Allium is a huge genus of flowering plants. Some of them are grown only for their blooms as ornamentals, while others, such as garlic, onions, leeks and chives, are cultivated for their edible shoots and bulbs.

Garlic / *Allium sativum*

🌱 OCT–FEB DIRECT

☀️ (RICH) H: 10–50CM 🧺 JUN–AUG

Garlic seems to be an ingredient in every dish I cook! It is easy to grow but does take up a bit of space as you need to grow a lot of plants if you want a decent harvest to store and use in winter. If space is an issue and you cannot dedicate a large bed for garlic alone, consider growing garlic interplanted between rows of carrots and salads where its sulphurous scent deters some pests. Garlic comes in two types: hardneck garlic, which produces larger and fewer cloves but does not store very long; and softneck garlic, which produces more tightly packed, smaller cloves and stores well. Garlic prefers sandy, well-drained, non-acidic, fertile soil and full sun. For wild garlic, see Gourmet Weeds on p64.

STARTING OFF Garlic needs a period of cold to produce good cloves. Plant individual garlic cloves in autumn/winter, pushing them into soft, sandy soil 2cm under the surface, 15cm apart. Garlic likes rich, free-draining soil, so incorporate plenty of compost into the bed before planting.

GROWING ON Garlic is pretty unfussy and only needs the odd weeding and watering in dry weather.

PESTS AND DISEASES Allium leaf miner and rust can both be an issue.

HARVEST Garlic is ready to harvest once its green stems have turned yellow. Lift the bulbs on a dry day and continue to dry further, laying them out in a single layer under the sun for a few hours. Plait the stems and hang in a dry, frost-free place out of direct sunlight and make sure there's a good airflow. Softneck varieties keep for up to a year.

Onion (bulb and bunching) / *Allium cepa* and *A. fistulosum* ↗

🌱 BULB: OCT–FEB INDOORS. BUNCHING: MAR–JUL DIRECT

☀️ (SANDY, POTASH RICH) H: 40CM–1M

🧺 BULB: JUN–AUG. BUNCHING: ALL YEAR

Bulb onions are much like garlic in their care requirements. They can take up a lot of space if you want a good harvest, but can also be interplanted and snuck into other beds as companion plants to deter certain pests such as carrot root fly. They can be plaited and stored for months, so are great to grow for a bumper end-of-summer harvest – if you have space for them. Pictured opposite is 'Pink Panther'.

Place the tray in a heated propagator or on a sunny windowsill. Plant out seedlings when they are 10cm high at a spacing of 5cm. To increase your harvest from the space, pull up every other plant to eat as a baby onion, allowing the others to grow on to full size. Bulb onions can also be grown from 'sets' bought online. Sets are small onions started off the previous year that can be planted in spring for an earlier harvest.

Bunching onions should be sown in their growing site by scattering seeds direct where you want them to grow.

GROWING ON Keep the area around bulb onions weed free and well watered in dry spells. Stop watering towards the end of summer to allow bulb onions to dry out for storage.

Bunching onions can be watered throughout the growing period to keep the stems supple and green.

PESTS AND DISEASES Allium leaf miner and rust can impact onions.

HARVEST Harvest bulb onions on a dry day in late summer when the leafy tops have begun to turn brown. Lay them out in the sun for a few hours and then plait into bunches for hanging. Bunching onions can be harvested whenever they are needed, either by cutting away some of the green growth (if harvested like this they will regrow a few more times) or by pulling up entire plants as salad onions.

Bunching onions are great! Otherwise known as spring onions, Welsh onions, green onions or even salad onions, most varieties of bunching onions are very little hassle. They can be planted at intervals throughout spring and most of summer – tuck them in along the edges of beds or in pots for a year-long harvest.

STARTING OFF Sow bulb onion seeds in late winter in either a propagation tray (at a distance of 2cm apart) or module tray (one seed per module).

Leafy brassicas

The *Brassica* genus spans a wide range of important culinary crops, including bok choy, cauliflower, broccoli, kale, cabbage, Brussels sprouts and kohlrabi, as well as some root crops such as turnips and radishes. For the purpose of this section we will focus on the leafy brassicas, *Brassica oleracea*.

All *B. oleracea* plants were selectively bred by humans from a single wild cabbage ancestor for certain key, edible features. For instance, kale was bred for its large, fan-like leaves, broccoli for its flower buds and Brussels sprouts for their lateral buds. Cabbage was also bred for its leaves, though unlike kale its tight-forming heads can be stored over winter.

Many brassicas take up a fair amount of room. If space is tight, note that all brassicas can be sown thickly and harvested as microgreens (see p74). Or they can be spaced at around 10cm apart and allowed to grow a few weeks beyond microgreen stage, then harvested as mini-but-whole brassica leaf heads when around 20–30cm high.

Most leafy brassicas require similar treatment, so here, to avoid repetition, are some general tips for growing them. You'll find specific care tips for a few particular forms on the following pages.

STARTING OFF Sow brassica seeds directly in their growing spot or in module trays in spring or late summer. Seedlings do not like extreme heat, so if sowing in module trays only keep them inside a greenhouse or cold frame if the temperature is cool. In warm springs and summer, keep baby brassica plants in a protected sunny spot outside. Plant out when seedlings reach 10–15cm.

GENERAL CARE It is important not to let brassica seedlings get pot bound. They do not like having their roots restricted and find it hard to bounce back once they've become stressed due to lack of space. If your final spot for brassicas is still full of summer veg, be sure to pot your seedlings on into larger pots regularly to avoid stressing them out. Brassicas have short root systems and, as they grow, stems can get long and top heavy. To prevent them falling over, earth up the stems with mounds of soil and stake the plants with a thick cane. Apart from netting and staking, brassicas don't require much special attention, though they benefit from the odd application of compost or manure.

PESTS AND DISEASES There is a long list of pests associated with brassicas that you need to fend off to get a decent crop. But it is well worth the effort for the bountiful and nutritious harvest you'll be rewarded with. Plus, the remedies are relatively simple and very effective.

All leafy brassicas should be protected from bird attack, especially when young. In winter, I do this by surrounding plants with sticks and twigs to create a natural barrier, reducing the need for netting. But in summer, smaller flying pests become evident and brassicas need to be netted. Several species of butterfly can cause severe damage to brassica crops. They lay their eggs on the leaves, and these hatch into very hungry caterpillars that can decimate plants in days or even hours. Another pest is whitefly. These tiny (1–2mm), white-winged insects congregate en masse on the underside of leaves. While they do not kill brassicas, they leave behind unsightly white marks that aren't very appetising.

Net plants with a fine-mesh netting to prevent pests landing. Cabbage root fly can be avoided by placing a collar of cut cardboard 20cm in circumference around the base of the plant – this prevents the female flies from laying their eggs. Nematode mixes can help prevent infestations of cabbage root fly. Protect against slugs and snails, particularly when plants are young.

← Broccoli / *Brassica oleracea* Italica Group

🫘 FEB–JUL ☀️ ◑ (RICH) H: 40CM–1.5M
🗓 FEB–APR AND JUL–OCT

Main stem broccoli is the common, large, green-headed broccoli that many of us are familiar with as it's sold in supermarkets. It is ready to harvest towards the end of summer and into autumn. Sprouting broccoli is a winter-hardy brassica that produces purple (pictured), white or green side shoots in spring, when not much else is cropping in the garden – a time that's known as 'the hungry gap'!

STARTING OFF See 'starting off' on p103.

GROWING ON Plant out seedlings at a spacing of 40–50cm. Water once a week in dry periods.

HARVEST For main stem broccoli, cut off full heads while they are still tight and firm. Side shoots will then appear and these can be harvested like sprouting broccoli. For sprouting broccoli, simply cut the stems as needed. To keep broccoli producing well, ensure that you harvest stems regularly so as not to allow the flower buds to open and set seed.

Cabbage / *Brassica oleracea* Capitata Group

🫘 SEE 'STARTING OFF' BELOW.

☀️ ◑ (RICH/FIRM) H: 20–50CM
🗓 ALL YEAR, DEPENDING ON TYPE

Cabbage may not seem like the most exciting vegetable, but I love it in all forms and add it to so many dishes, from soups and pickles to salads. Its amazing leaves are big enough to be stuffed with rice and veggies or turned into cabbage summer rolls. Cabbages do take up a lot of space, though, and don't do well in pots. They prefer a large

Autumn cabbages often form large heads so need a little wider spacing. Sow direct in mid-spring or start off in pots and harvest before the first frosts.

Winter cabbages form large heads and needs greater spacing than spring and summer cabbages. Sow them direct in April/May or start them off in pots and plant out when large enough to handle. Winter cabbages are usually frost tolerant and can stand out in the garden all winter until you are ready to harvest. But if your area experiences harsh frosts, it may be worth bringing them inside for storage.

GROWING ON Cabbages love rich, firm soil. When transplanting, firm down the compost in the bed first and firm in seedlings well. Different cabbages require different spacing – some are compact, some are huge.

HARVEST Harvest time changes depending on the type you're growing (see 'starting off'). Most cabbages are ready to harvest after four to eight months from sowing, when they have reached the desired size and firm heads have formed. To harvest, cut stems with a sharp knife.

bed in full sun. They are categorised into groups defined by when they are harvested, so you'll find spring, summer, autumn and winter varieties. Spring and summer cabbages keep for a few weeks once harvested and autumn and winter varieties can often be stored in their raw form for up to six months in the right conditions (cool, dark, dry), so you don't have to worry too much about a glut.

STARTING OFF Spring cabbages usually form dense, pointed heads. Sow direct or in pots in mid- to late summer for overwintering. Harvest from spring to midsummer.

Summer cabbages are bred to withstand summer heat and are sown in late winter/early spring indoors. Plant out once frosts have passed.

Kale / *Brassica oleracea* Acephala Group ↗

🌱 MAR–JUN OR LATE AUG–SEP

☀️ ◑ (ANY) H: 20CM–2M 🧺 ALL YEAR

Kale is likely the most ancient of the cultivated brassicas, grown by early Europeans for at least 4,000 years – it's thought to have spread with the Roman Empire. My love for kale runs deep for many reasons: it is easy to cultivate, productive, highly nutritious, beautiful and grows year-round, with many varieties surviving even hard frosts. There are tons of different cultivars, but they generally fall into three categories: flat leaf, curly leaf (such as the 'Dwarf Green Curled', pictured) and bumpy leaf (known as cavolo nero or Tuscan kale).

Kale tends to grow tall and narrow and produces well, so you can get by with just one or two plants for a small family. Walking stick kale (*B. o.* var. *palmifolia*) is a massive variety that grows up to 2.5m tall, but doesn't take up more ground space than smaller kales. Perpetual kale (*B. o.* var. *ramosa*) or tree kale can be grown over years and years as a perennial crop if you continue to cut any flower spikes that form.

STARTING OFF See 'starting off' on p103.

GROWING ON Plant kale out in its final growing position at a distance of 40–50cm. Incorporate plenty of well-rotted compost. I sow kale in late summer/early autumn so I have a good supply of green leafy veg throughout winter. Kale sown at this time is slow to grow and can take up a lot of valuable bed space, so I tend to grow it in pots to reach a good size while I wait for other summer veg such as tomatoes and squash to finish their life cycle and clear their beds.

Then once the beds are clear, I plant it in the ground for winter.

HARVEST Kale leaves can be repeatedly harvested throughout the growing season. The plant grows tall, sprouting new layers of edible leaves as it reaches towards the sky. Snap off the lowest leaves and allow the top of the plant to continue to grow. To get the most from kale, continue to harvest the leaves until the plant begins to set flowers, then cut the flowers to eat as you would sprouting broccoli. You can continue to harvest flower stalks until the flowers that are produced become tiny. Generally kale plants let you know when they will no longer produce leaves and flower stalks by slowing down their growth and eventually succumbing to disease such as powdery mildew.

Perennial vegetables

Perennial vegetables are ones that come back year on year. They are great for the low-maintenance gardener as they usually require very little fussing once the plant is established.

Asparagus / *Asparagus officinalis* ↘

🌱 MAR ☀️ ◑ (RICH/FREE DRAINING)

H: 20CM–2M 🧺 APR–JUN

Growing asparagus takes a little patience but is incredibly easy. You can start it off from seed, but most people grow it from dormant roots known as crowns. Once crowns are in the ground they need to be left for a year or two before any spears can be harvested to allow the plants to establish. Once settled, they will crop for years to come. It is best to choose an all-male cultivar that produces stronger spears. If any plants grow to produce red berries, you have a female in the mix – remove these spears if they form by chopping them at the base. Asparagus needs light, well-drained soil and doesn't do well in pots. A raised bed all to itself is ideal – it will crop in that spot for 15–20 years!

STARTING OFF Plant asparagus crowns in early spring by digging plenty of compost into the bed and creating a shallow ditch with a slight mound in the middle (pictured below). Lay the octopus-like legs over each side of the mound, spacing them 30–40cm apart. Cover with 5cm compost, leaving the centre of the crown slightly exposed. Keep beds well weeded and well watered throughout the growing season.

GROWING ON Asparagus benefits from general fertiliser applied in early spring and again in midsummer. Mulch around crowns with compost in late autumn/ early winter. Otherwise, you can simply let them do their thing. It really is that easy. To increase your asparagus plants, divide established crowns in late winter or early spring; this should

Opposite Mashua (*Tropaeolum tuberosum*)

only be done every three years or so, to avoid exhausting the plant.

PESTS AND DISEASES Check plants for asparagus beetle from late spring onwards and pick off any larvae or beetles by hand. Protect from slugs and snails.

HARVEST Don't harvest any spears in the first year; instead, let plants grow their ferny foliage (pictured opposite on p110) and photosynthesise to give the root stock plenty of energy to establish. The plants grow huge and may need staking at this point. In autumn, once the plants have turned fully brown and all the goodness has travelled back down into the crowns, cut back the dead plant to 10cm above the ground. In year two you can harvest 50 per cent of the spears by cutting with a sharp knife 3cm above the soil. Allow the remaining spears to grow as in year one. From year three onwards you can harvest all of the spears as they grow until mid-June. Allow remaining spears to grow into ferny plants, just as you did in years one and two. This gives the plant a chance to build energy reserves for the following year.

Chinese artichoke / *Stachys affinis* ↗

🌡 OCT–APR ☀️ ◑ (ANY)
H: UP TO 50CM 🧺 OCT–FEB

Chinese artichoke is a rampant little grower. It is not an artichoke at all, rather it's a member of the mint (*Lamiaceae*) family – and it certainly

grows like mint, spreading like wildfire wherever it's planted. For this reason, grow it in large pots or a dedicated raised bed. This plant puts on lots of lush leaf growth, but it is the small, knobbly, bobbly, white tubers that are harvested to eat. These are crunchy and fresh and mild in flavour. They can be eaten raw, cooked or pickled. They are pictured at the top of the image on p151.

STARTING OFF Plant tubers during their dormant months between October and April. Plant each tuber 7–10cm deep, 30–40cm apart.

GROWING ON This plant is not fussy at all. Give it plenty of water in dry spells and it will flourish.

PESTS AND DISEASES Young plants can be subject to slug attack, but other than that they are relatively pest-free and robust.

HARVEST The top growth is frost tender and will die down in the winter months, indicating that the tubers are ready to harvest. Lift tubers as you need them throughout their dormant season as they do not store well once out of the ground. Any tubers left in the ground will grow again next year.

Globe artichoke / *Cynara cardunculus* Scolymus Group

🌱 🛠 MAR–APR ☀️ 🌓 (RICH/FREE DRAINING)
H: UP TO 2M 🧺 JUN–SEP

Artichokes are perennial plants from the *Asteraceae* family; they are related to dandelions and thistles, which you can see in their flower and leaf shape. I love adding artichokes to perennial borders where their architectural beauty shines. They are also great for interplanting with other edibles to create layers of planting, so you can avoid having a low-growing vegetable patch. Opt for taller perennial plants such as fruit bushes or climbing plants such as mashua (*Tropaeolum tuberosum*), which can intertwine up the artichoke stems. Artichokes are great for filling gaps in borders as they require little input, but produce plenty of beauty and edible goodness.

STARTING OFF Artichokes can be grown from small plants or from seed in early spring. Start seeds off indoors in modules or individual pots to protect from critters and give them a head start. Transplant to their final growing space when seedlings have at least five true leaves. Remember these are perennials, so they will grow in the same spot for many years to come. Add plenty of compost to the growing bed and plant out seedlings at a spacing of 60–80cm.

GROWING ON Artichokes are pretty easy going. They need watering in dry weather and enjoy a good top-dressing with compost in early spring. Divide plants every two to three years to give old plants space and create new plants for the coming years.

PESTS AND DISEASES Artichokes are pretty hardy once established. Young plants are prone to slug attack. Aphids can be a problem too.

HARVEST Most artichokes produce multiple heads with the central stalk maturing first. Harvest heads one at a time as they reach 8–10cm diameter by cutting them at an angle with a sharp knife or secateurs.

Jerusalem artichoke / *Helianthus tuberosus* ↗

🛠 MAR–APR ☀️ 🌓 (RICH/FREE DRAINING)
H: UP TO 2M 🧺 JUN–SEP

Jerusalem artichokes or 'sunchokes' are large, unfussy plants of the *Asteraceae* family that produce masses of edible tubers. They are the ultimate lazy gardener's friend and grow in

pretty much any soil with almost no input. They even grow in shady areas, though they produce much better in full sun. They grow tall and spread well so allow them plenty of space. Because they are so big, I tend to plant them around the edges of perennial borders rather than in veg beds.

STARTING OFF Jerusalem artichokes are started from tubers that are planted in spring. Prepare the bed by adding plenty of compost. Plant at a depth of 10–15cm, 30cm apart.

GROWING ON Jerusalem artichokes do not require much attention. They are quite drought tolerant but need watering in very dry spells. They do grow very tall so may need staking in exposed areas. Cut back dead material once the plant has turned completely

brown in winter. At this point you can harvest the tubers or leave them in the ground until you need them – in fact they store better underground than in the pantry. Just be sure to harvest them before they begin to sprout again in the spring.

PESTS AND DISEASES Jerusalem artichokes are pretty tough and resistant to diseases. The young shoots can be munched by slugs in wet springs, but the plants usually recover and go on to grow big and strong.

HARVEST Dig up tubers in midwinter once all of the above-ground parts have died back. Be sure to plant a few back in the bed for next year's crop.

Herbs

If you can grow only one thing, let it be herbs! For flavour and value for time, money and space, herbs are the ideal edible garden plants. They take up little space, are incredibly low maintenance and attract beneficial pollinators. Many, like rosemary, thyme, mint and lemon balm, are perennial, meaning you need to plant them just once, reaping the rewards for years to come.

Most of our well-known culinary herbs are in the mint family (*Lamiaceae*) and require nothing more than sunshine and a gentle prune, which they get when you harvest them anyway. Most herbs can be harvested all year round if grown indoors on a sunny windowsill, but they will grow very slowly when sunshine levels are low. For this reason, take your main harvests in summer when growth is bountiful and dry them for later use.

Opposite A bed of mixed herbs **Above** Eau de Cologne mint (*Mentha × piperita* f. *citrata* 'Basil')

Basil / *Ocimum basilicum*
There are so many exciting basil varieties, but few are available in the supermarket. Thai basil has an aniseed flavour, Greek basil is small-leaved and probably the most hardy, and lemon basil has a citrus twang. Then there are purple and blue-purple basils, which have a deep camphor aroma.
Sow basil from seed in spring and summer in a seed tray or medium-sized pot aiming for about 1cm spacing. Cover the seeds with 0.5cm of fine soil or vermiculite and keep warm until they germinate. The main thing to keep basil plants happy is to give them plenty of sunshine and harvest properly. People often pick off the biggest leaves from the bottom or middle of the stems, leaving just the very smallest leaves at the tips. This leaves the plant long and lanky and not too happy. Instead, cut the growing tip of the plant, cutting its stem just above a pair of leaves. This encourages the plant to bush out.

Lemon balm / *Melissa officinalis* →

Lemon balm makes a beautiful herbal tea or cordial and is a joy to brush past on a summer's day, filling the air with citrusy aromas. It makes a great companion plant as many insects enjoy its nectar, which helps with pollination. It grows well from seed but is easiest to grow from a cutting or young plant.

Once you have lemon balm in the garden it starts popping up everywhere, spreading by both runners and seeds, forming lush bushes of fragrant greenery. If you want to keep it confined to a certain area, cut the flower stems off as they form, though it's worth keeping a few stray flowers for the beautiful butterflies and bees that they attract.

Cut lemon balm leaves whenever you need them and use fresh. Its aromatic oils are volatile and don't 'stick' well in the drying process. Lemon balm can be prone to powdery mildew in dry weather: keep it well watered and cut down affected stems to the ground to encourage healthy new growth.

Lemon verbena / *Aloysia citrodora* ↗

This beautiful plant can grow quite large, reaching heights of 2.5m. It has lime-green, lemon-scented leaves, which can be used to infuse teas. The long flower spikes attract various beneficial insects. It is an attractive addition to any mixed border or bed and can be grown in large pots. Don't be disheartened when lemon verbena drops its leaves in autumn and winter; it is a deciduous shrub and will emerge again in spring. In colder climates it may need some protection from harsh frosts and is best planted in a sheltered, sunny position. To keep it in good shape, it needs a late summer or early autumn prune: cut it down to one or two buds above the woody growth.

↙ Mint / *Mentha* spp.

Mint is amazing as it is so resilient. It spreads like wildfire and makes great ground cover. If you don't want it taking over, grow it in a container as it spreads from seed and root. It will naturally die back in cold winters and pop up again, growing with full force from mid-spring. Cut mint down to ground level in late autumn as leaves begin to brown. This will encourage better growth in spring and help to limit disease. Harvest whenever you need it: cutting generously promotes new growth. Like many plants in the mint family, it can be started from seed but grows much more readily from plants or cuttings.

Oregano / *Origanum vulgare* ↑

Pungent and aromatic, oregano is a non-fussy plant. It is drought tolerant and will survive most British winters, especially if grown in a sheltered spot. It loves full sun and a good haircut during its growing season, so chop off sprigs as you need them as it will encourage new green growth. Leave a small part of the plant to go to flower as the bees love it. Cut oregano back in late summer, trimming to a few buds above the woodier growth. Dry the green cuttings and flowers for use throughout the winter months.

Parsley / *Petroselinum crispum* ↑
Parsley is so underrated: if grown as a houseplant on a sunny windowsill or in a greenhouse it will stay green and ready to harvest all winter. One variety I love is the big-leaved 'Italian Giant', which I have found even overwinters outside in a mild winter. Parsley is best started from seed (any time indoors, but growth is best in spring and summer), in a pot at a spacing of 1cm. Cover with a sprinkling of soil.

Harvest the outer leaves whenever you need them, leaving the growing centre uncut to encourage growth. If stressed due to heat or drought, parsley can bolt: if this happens, cut off any flower stems and keep plants well watered to prolong leaf production.

Rosemary / *Salvia rosmarinus* ↑
Rosemary is a staple of any edible garden. It is a perennial plant that requires very little care to keep it happy. It does best in full sun with free-draining soil as waterlogged soil can cause its roots to rot. It loves a good prune towards the end of summer once the flowers begin to fade. To prune, cut most of this year's green growth back, but do not cut into old wood. All trimmings can be dried for use throughout the winter months. Although rosemary can be harvested

fresh all year round, it will grow very slowly over the winter months.

Sage / *Salvia officinalis*

As with many herbs, this is a low-maintenance and beautiful, aromatic plant in the mint family. Sage comes in many interesting forms other than the standard green garden sage. Colours range from silver-green to yellow and even purple. There are also variegated cultivars such as 'Icterina' and 'Tricolor'. Sage requires a prune in late summer (remove spent flower heads at this time) and then again in the spring to encourage fresh, vibrant growth. Do not let sage sit in waterlogged soil as it will cause roots to rot. If planting in clay soil, it is worth digging in some sand and loam for added drainage.

Thyme / *Thymus* spp. ↗

Thyme is generally listed as frost tolerant, but I lose a plant or two every year if I leave it outside over winter. I prefer to grow it in a polytunnel or a pot that I can bring inside when it's frosty. Common thyme (*Thymus vulgaris*) is a great all-rounder, but there are plenty of varieties offering a range of flavours and variegated colours. Three of my favourites are: 'Silver Queen', a variegated, compact,

bushy form with crimson stems; lemon thyme (*T. × citriodorus*), an upright hybrid with variegated leaves and a strong lemon scent; and wild thyme (*T. serpyllum*), a creeper that forms dense mats of scented leaves and flowers. Wild thyme is very hardy and makes a beautiful addition to rockeries, wildflower lawns and anywhere you want to add some ground cover.

Thyme is best grown from a plant or cutting, as seed germination can be sporadic and seedlings take a while to get going. Harvest when it puts on plenty of fresh green growth in summer. Cutting regularly encourages new growth and better plant shape.

Fruit

Most fruiting bushes and trees are easy to grow and require little attention other than pruning once or twice a year and the odd bit of mulch. They produce well over years and years and provide a great harvest throughout summer and autumn.

← Apples / *Malus domestica*

NOV–MAR ☀ (MOST)
H: UP TO 10M 🧺 AUG–NOV

No edible garden is complete without an apple tree. They provide great habitats for all manner of creatures, shade on the hottest days and, importantly, an abundance of fruit.

Different varieties ripen at different stages and all apples will benefit from having another variety to pollinate with. If your garden is close to many other gardens, pollination probably won't be a problem as apple trees are common. If your garden is remote, consider buying a 'family' variety – a tree that has several varieties grafted onto one root stock, which means it will self-pollinate. If you have space, go for at least two varieties in a standard (a tree with a single stem at 1.8m) or half-standard (a tree with a single stem at 1.2–1.5m) tree. If space is tight, go for a dwarf bush variety or one specifically bred for growing in pots. Alternatively, try an espalier – a variety you can train to grow flat against a wall or trellis. Buy apple trees from a reputable supplier

to ensure they are from good stock and disease free. There are so many interesting ones out there, from floral eating apples such as 'Rosette' to sour, crisp cooking apples such as 'Howgate Wonder'.

STARTING OFF Plant out trees in their dormancy in winter or early spring. Dig a hole, three to five times the size of the root ball, and mix in plenty of compost. Place the tree in the hole and fill it in while supporting the trunk –don't bury the trunk deeper than it was in the pot, as this can cause it to rot. Firm in well with your foot and water well.

GROWING ON Apples require little attention. Give them plentiful water in times of drought and apply a compost mulch in winter and spring.

PRUNING Apple trees need to be pruned twice per year: once in summer (July to September) and again in winter when they are dormant (November to February). The summer prune is to remove the water shoots and encourage fruiting. Water shoots are the long, flexible green shoots that appear over summer. These sap energy from the fruit-giving parts of the tree so are best removed at their base with a clean cut as close to the branch as possible (unless you want to keep it to create a pleasing tree shape).

The winter prune is done to keep a good size, shape and air spacing between branches. Aim to remove 10 to 20 per cent of the canopy each year. Using sharp secateurs or a pruning saw, cut away any branches that grow inwards or cross over one another. This is to stop rubbing and prevent disease. Tree pruning can be a daunting task and one that is hard to learn from books. There are tons of great online tutorials and in-person orchard workshops out there. I'd highly recommend learning in practice.

PESTS AND DISEASES There are unfortunately many diseases that affect apple trees – too many to go into detail here. One common problem to look out for is canker, which presents as raised, flaky patches on the bark of a tree, often with a sunken middle. It is a fungal infection that occasionally causes developing fruits to rot and drop. Not much can be done about canker other than cutting out infected branches during the tree's dormant period. A small amount of canker is common and usually the tree will survive, but it will be weakened over time by the infection.

Squirrels love apples: these pesky little creatures nab a large portion of my apples every year. My garden is located in woodland so they are always out in full force. I hang old CDs and wind chimes in the trees, which does deter them somewhat. Also spraying developing fruits with chilli spray (see

p150) can put squirrels off. Codling moth can also be an issue.

HARVEST Early ripening apples will be ready to harvest from late summer but the main harvest for most varieties is early autumn. It's best to pick apples before they drop to the ground to avoid bruised fruit. To harvest, clasp the apple and twist it: if it comes away from the tree easily it is ready; if not, leave it for a little longer.

Blueberries / *Vaccinium* spp. ↓
🌡 NOV–MAR ☀ ◗ (ACIDIC)
H: UP TO 1.5M 🧺 JUL–SEP

Blueberries are beautiful plants that make sweet, lantern-shaped, creamy flowers in late spring and put on a gorgeous display in autumn as leaves start to turn bright red. They

thrive in acidic soil so are perfect for a forest garden. If you have alkaline soil, consider growing blueberries in a raised bed or container, using ericaceous soil as a growing medium. Alternatively, dress beds with coffee grounds and plenty of composted pine bark (available in bags at garden centres) to lower the pH.

STARTING OFF Buy blueberry bushes from a reputable supplier. Two-year-old plants are best as they will fruit in the same year. Alternatively, if you know someone with a bush, ask for a cutting and grow on for a year or two. Avoid planting if the ground is frozen.

GROWING ON Apply a well-rotted, pine-bark mulch or layer of ericaceous soil in summer to prevent moisture loss. Water well as the flowers begin to set to ensure good fruiting.

PESTS AND DISEASES Protect from birds with netting, branches (to deter birds landing) or a fruit cage.

HARVEST Pick berries as they ripen.

Pinkcurrant 'Gloire de Sablons'

Currants / *Ribes rubrum* and *R. nigrum* ↗

🌡 NOV–MAR ☀ ◑ (ACIDIC)

H: UP TO 2M 🧺 JUN–AUG

Currants come in a range of colours, from red, pink and white to black – well, more dark purple. They are perennial bushes that fruit for up to 15 years, so choose their spot wisely. When not in fruit, most currant bushes look the same, so it is hard to tell red from white currants until the berries emerge, but you can recognise a blackcurrant bush as its leaves smell like blackcurrant. Wild currant bushes grow on the edges of woodland and can handle dappled shade, though they produce bigger, more abundant fruits if grown in full sun. They also like a rich, free-draining and, importantly, slightly acidic soil, so will benefit from a pine-bark mulch in alkaline soils.

STARTING OFF Currants often do not produce fruits for the first two years, so try to acquire more mature plants if possible. Before planting, dig plenty of compost into the bed. Bury plants 3–5cm deeper than they were originally planted to encourage strong root systems. A final spacing of 1m between plants is sufficient, but not necessary if they are growing in a polyculture bed with lots of different plants as allies.

GROWING ON In early spring, apply a high-potassium feed such as comfrey (see p134) to encourage flower and fruit growth. In hot weather, mulch with leaf mulch or well-rotted woodchip to prevent moisture loss.

PRUNING Cut back any dead stems and plant material in winter once the plant has lost all of its leaves. Fruits are borne on last year's growth so prune stems lightly, unless growth is poor, in which case prune around half the stems to ground level to encourage healthy growth in the spring. Currants are incredibly easy to propagate from cuttings. Simply stick the chopped stems in the ground or in pots after pruning to form roots and come to life as a whole new plant in the spring (see p138 for more on cuttings).

PESTS AND DISEASES The number-one pest for currants is birds, which love to feed on the sweet berries. Cover fruiting plants with netting or protect with twigs and branches to prevent birds from landing. Alternatively, grow currants in a fruit cage.

HARVEST Pick individual fruits or entire trusses as they ripen in summer. The fruiting season is short but very productive in happy plants.

Plums / *Prunus domestica* →

🌡 NOV–MAR ☀ (MOST) H: UP TO 6M
🧺 AUG–NOV

Most commercially available plums do not compare to varieties you can grow at home. Plums tend to be fairly soft fruits and so cannot be transported well, meaning that the varieties we have access to in the shops are harder and, I find, less flavoursome. Homegrown plums and greengages can be so tender that they literally slip off the tree into your hand like honey. If you have the space, I urge you to try a super-tender, sweet variety such as 'Cambridge Gage'.

STARTING OFF Obtain baby plum trees from a reputable supplier to ensure disease-free stock. Plums are grown in a similar way to apples (see p121 for more planting tips). In late autumn to early spring, dig a large hole and fill with lots of compost, plant the plum tree in, backfill and water well.

GROWING ON Water young trees regularly and deeply in dry weather. Mulch twice a year: once in spring and again in late autumn.

squirrels also like to nibble on fruits, often before they have even matured. Spray with chilli spray (see p150) and net some fruiting branches to protect enough fruits for you.

HARVEST Plums are ripe when they feel soft. Pick them as needed or pick slightly unripe and ripen in a fruit bowl.

Raspberries / *Rubus* spp. ↓

🌡 NOV–MAR   ☀ ◐   (RICH)
H: UP TO 2M   🧺 JUN–OCT

Raspberries come in summer-fruiting and autumn-fruiting varieties depending on when the fruits ripen. If you have space, try growing a mixture to get a longer harvesting season.

Like many fruiting plants, wild raspberries grow at the edge of woodland so tend to like slightly

PRUNING Plums are borne on one- or two-year-old wood. It is best to prune young trees lightly in spring to encourage vigorous growth. Prune established trees in summer: the main objective is to maintain the tree's shape and remove any dead wood. Cut all growth back by about a third, cutting just above a leaf node. Don't worry if you cut away a few developing fruits, this may even help the tree by focusing its energy on a smaller number of fruits that will grow bigger and juicier. Avoid pruning stone fruit trees when they are in their dormant stage, to avoid infection.

PESTS AND DISEASES Plum maggots can eat through the inside of fruits before you get a look-in. Consider using pheromone traps if this becomes a problem for your tree. Birds and

acidic soil and can grow in partial shade, though produce more fruits in full sun. They can also grow in pots, though you need quite a few plants (five to ten) to get a worthwhile harvest – one that will make it back to the kitchen, rather than get eaten straight from the plant. Bear in mind that raspberries are closely related to brambles and multiply very well. You can start one year with just one or two canes and have ten to 15 by the following year. Golden raspberries such as 'All Gold' are wonderful and rarely found in shops.

STARTING OFF Plant raspberry crowns in their dormant state during winter at a distance of 45cm apart and 1.5m between rows. They love rich, free-draining soil so add plenty of compost to the beds before planting them up.

GROWING ON Lift any suckers that pop up between rows and replant. They do multiply well, so if you have space, try starting a new bed or consider giving some away. Mulch around with compost and apply a liquid feed as flowers set in. It is especially important to keep raspberries well watered as the flower buds begin to appear.

PRUNING Summer-fruiting raspberries may need support and tying into a frame as they can get a little sprawly. This also helps you to distinguish between the new canes and the old ones. Summer-fruiting raspberries are pruned in late summer after they have fruited. They form fruits on last year's growth so it is important to only cut the canes that have already produced fruit that year, leaving newer growth on the plant.

Autumn-fruiting varieties produce flowering, fruiting canes in one growing season, so cut all of them down to ground level in winter once they have fruited.

PESTS AND DISEASES Raspberries can be affected by various viruses that can cause an array of different symptoms, mostly affecting leaf and fruit vigour and production including browning or yellowing leaves, curled leaf edges, dry, crumbly fruit and dying back of entire stems. If you spot any of these symptoms and have ruled out other causes (such as drought or insect attack) then it is likely a viral problem. Not much can be done other than to dig up and destroy the affected raspberry plants and create a new bed with new plants. Be sure to protect ripening berries from hungry birds. The best way is to use a fruit cage; alternatively, drape some fine mesh netting over the plants during fruiting season.

HARVEST Fruits are ready when they are easy to pull off.

Rhubarb / *Rheum* × *hybridum* →

CROWNS: OCT–MAR. PLANTS: APR–JUN

☀ ◑ (ACIDIC) H: UP TO 1M 🧺 MAR–JUL

Rhubarb is a beautiful, resilient plant that requires minimal effort. Its large, green leaves and red stems (not technically fruits) look gorgeous in a sunny spot in the garden. Rhubarb can be 'forced', which involves excluding light from the developing shoots by covering them with a vessel – traditionally an old terracotta chimney pot, but a large bucket will do. Cover them in early spring just as the buds appear on the crowns and leave the covers in place until the stems are a desirable length, usually 40cm or more. This creates longer, paler, more tender stems that can be harvested earlier than rhubarb left to mature at its own pace.

I love the varieties 'Timperley Early', which produces stalks from early April onwards, and 'Victoria', which is very heavy cropping, producing masses of chunky stems.

STARTING OFF Rhubarb can be started from seed but is much better grown from established crowns bought from a reputable supplier. You can also buy it as an actively growing plant for planting whenever it is in leaf. Add plenty of compost to the growing bed and plant in shallow holes, being careful not to bury the centres of the crowns as this can cause them to rot. Space plants 75cm–1m apart as they can become huge!

GROWING ON Mulch around rhubarb plants with compost in early spring, being careful not to cover crowns. Divide crowns every five years or so to multiply your plants and prevent overcrowding. Do this by digging up crowns when they are dormant in winter and splitting them in half (or quarters for big plants) with a spade. Rhubarb plants are thirsty and need regular watering in dry weather.

PESTS AND DISEASES Crown rot is caused by fungi or bacteria, particularly in

plants grown in soil that does not drain freely. It causes crowns, stems and leaves to rot and die. Ensure adequate drainage by incorporating leaf mulch and sand in the rhubarb bed before planting in clay or claggy soils. Slugs can eat young leaves but usually the plants become so large that this does not cause too much of a problem.

HARVEST Pick forced rhubarb stems from March. Unforced rhubarb comes into season April to July, depending on the variety. As tempting as the rhubarb may be, stop harvesting in July to allow stems to die back and feed the crowns for next year's growth.

Strawberries / *Fragaria* spp. →

🌱 MAR–APR ☀️ ◑ (RICH/FREE DRAINING)
H: UP TO 30CM 🧺 JUN–OCT

Strawberries are the epitome of the summer garden. There is nothing quite like taking a walk around your plot on a hazy morning and nibbling a few sweet strawberries on the way. It doesn't matter how many times I do it, it always feels like a treat. Wild strawberries grow just about anywhere and make excellent ground cover for shady areas under trees and along paths. They don't produce as much fruit as cultivated strawberries, but they are intensely flavoursome and the hunt to find a ripe one among the foliage is well worth it. Cultivated strawberries are bigger, juicier and produce more reliably. Different varieties ripen at different times, so consider growing

a few types to extend the harvesting season. Each plant produces fruits well for three to five years, after which production slows significantly.

STARTING OFF Strawberries are best grown from bought plants or runners. Enrich your growing bed with plenty of homemade compost and place plants 30–40cm apart in spring.

GROWING ON Feed plants with liquid fertiliser as flower buds begin to grow. As the fruits form, protect them from rotting on the moist ground by spreading a layer of straw around their base (hence the name 'strawberry'). Strawberries produce runners – baby plants borne on stems from the mother plant. When they have contact with the soil they form roots, and can then be cut from the main plant to create a whole new plant. Producing runners takes energy from the mother plant and so they can be cut away to focus the energy on fruiting. Alternatively, you can pot them up and grow them on to increase crop size or replenish old stock.

PESTS AND DISEASES All manner of critters will be in competition for the strawberry harvest, including nature's most cunning thief, the squirrel. Protect fruiting plants with netting to deter birds and rodents and apply chilli spray (see p150) regularly. Slugs and snails are often a problem too.

HARVEST Pick as they ripen.

04

Care
Learn to care for your crops and harvests

Fertilisers and soil conditioners

Fertilisers are concentrated sources of plant nutrients. There are tons of different fertilisers out there: liquid feeds, manures, granules and pellets. They aren't usually necessary if you have good soil with plenty of homemade compost dug in, but they can help prevent and treat nutrient deficiency in plants and encourage plants to produce more abundantly.

FEEDING YOUR PLANTS

Most fertilisers are based around three major plant nutrients:

N – Nitrogen (for healthy leaf growth)
P – Phosphorus (for healthy root and shoot growth)
K – Potassium (for healthy flower and fruit production)

Fertilisers can be split into two main categories: artificial and organic. Artificial (inorganic) fertilisers are available from garden centres, but I only use organic fertilisers that come from plant or animal sources. These include ones I make myself from comfrey and nettle plants (see p134 and p135).

Opposite Comfrey 'Bocking 14' (*Symphytum × uplandicum*)

Soil conditioners improve soil structure by increasing aeration, improving drainage, balancing pH and boosting nutrient availability. There are dozens of types, but I prefer ones that I can make at home, such as homemade compost or leaf mould.

Leaf mould This contains very few nutrients but is an excellent soil conditioner, helping to break down heavy clay soils or add structure to sandy soils. If you have trees in your garden, collect leaves in autumn and stuff them into old compost bags or pile them up in the corner of your garden, using netting to pen them in. In 12–18 months, the leaves will have rotted down into leaf mould (also known as leaf mulch) and can be used on beds.

Compost Homemade compost is by far my favourite garden fertiliser and soil conditioner. See p51 to learn more.

Lime Common garden lime (calcium carbonate) is ground limestone you can buy from garden centres and it helps to balance acidic soils. When soils are too acidic, plants cannot access nutrients. Check your soil pH (see p20) – if it is acidic, add one trowel-sized scoop of lime per square metre and dig in well. This is best done before planting as direct contact with lime can damage plants. Always wear protective gloves and do not breathe in the particles.

Manure I have moved away from animal fertilisers and soil conditioners, mainly in favour of plant-based ones that I can produce from things growing in my garden. But manure does deserve a mention. It's an excellent soil conditioner and is also rich in NPK and other trace elements essential for soil health. You can add a layer – apply between 3cm and 10cm – and dig into beds before planting or use it as a mulch around established plants. Don't use fresh manure – only use well-rotted manure that has been composted for a minimum of 12 months (24 is better) and make sure you buy from a reputable source, as some manures can be contaminated with herbicides.

Alfalfa pellets I used to use chicken manure pellets in abundance until I heard about these plant-based ones. If your compost pile isn't up and running yet and you need an instant fertiliser ASAP, try alfalfa pellets. Alfalfa pellets are better known as an animal fodder for horses and cows, but they are also an excellent addition to garden soil. They have a balanced NPK ratio and are slow releasing. Add a handful or two per square metre and dig in. Alternatively, sprinkle a fine layer in the hole before planting larger plants to give them instant access to nutrients through their roots.

Seaweed feed A concentrated liquid that can be used as a multipurpose feed for a wide range of plants. You can buy it readymade or make your own in much the same way as comfrey and nettle feed (see below). You need to soak the seaweed first and rinse away the salt.

Comfrey and nettle food Liquid food is easily made from these plants. Comfrey (*Symphytum × uplandicum*) is high in potassium while nettles (*Urtica*) are high in nitrogen. Both plants are incredibly easy to grow – so easy they are considered weeds. If you have the space, allow a small patch to grow in an unused part of the garden for a constant supply in the warmer months. If you are worried about them spreading, grow them in containers. See opposite for instructions on homemade plant food.

HOMEMADE PLANT FOOD

Plants can feed other plants, and two fantastic examples are comfrey (rich in potassium to boost fruiting) and nettles (a good source of nitrogen for healthy leaf growth). You can make separate comfrey and nettle feeds (nettle is best in its early stages of growth) or combine them together to make an all-purpose feed.

- Wear gloves to harvest nettles and comfrey (you can include stems and flowers or simply take the leaves). Chop up the plant material. Aim for about 1kg of plant material, but you can adjust the quantities of water if you have less.
- Fill a large bucket or lidded container with the plant material. Weigh it down with a brick or stone.
- Cover with rain water (or regular tap water if you don't have rain water). You'll need around 10 litres of water. Cover the bucket or put the lid on the container.

- Let the mixture sit for four to six weeks until it becomes a stinky, gooey mess.
- Strain off the liquid and put the sloppy 'solids' on the compost heap or dig it into beds in the same way you would manure (before planting out seedlings). Store the liquid in a lidded container as it really does stink.
- To use as a liquid fertiliser, dilute one part feed to ten parts water.

Mulch

Mulch is a layer of organic matter placed on growing beds or around plants to suppress weed growth, improve water retention and add nutrients. It can be as simple as piling some fallen leaves on an empty bed in autumn to rot down over winter. The worms will thank you for it by aerating the soil as they pop up to the surface to drag down the layer of mulch over time. Other mulches include grass clippings, which are high in nitrogen, sheep's wool, mushroom compost, homemade compost, straw and well-rotted manure. Mulches can also help to regulate soil pH. For instance, using pine bark around fruit bushes helps with acidity.

A pen to collect leaves to turn into leaf mould

WHEN TO MULCH

Plants benefit from mulch at any time of year. The problem is usually having enough to go around! Nitrogen- and nutrient-rich mulches such as well-rotted manure and compost are generally used in spring, a few weeks before planting out to give the soil a boost. Mulch is then applied again in autumn after the bulk of the summer harvest is over. Hungry fruiting plants such as tomatoes and squash happily take a compost mulch at any time in their growing season. But leafy greens may bolt in the hotter months if too much nitrogen is applied. This is when carbon-rich mulches such as leaf mould (see p133) are great.

HOW THICKLY TO APPLY

A general rule when applying mulch is to add a 5cm layer all over the planting area. Alternatively, just place mulch around the base of a plant, making a ring around it in a doughnut shape to avoid smothering the stem or leaves.

TO DIG OR NOT TO DIG

The no-dig method of gardening is exactly as it sounds: it involves doing very little or no digging/turning over of earth. Practising no-dig helps to maintain the structural integrity of soil, as excessive digging can break up the webs of fungi, mycelium and other microbes in the soil that keep it fertile (see p33 for more on no-dig beds).

Watering

People often ask me 'how much do you water this plant?'. That is a difficult question to answer. It depends on many factors including: what kind of soil you have; how sunny your growing spot is; whether you mulch the soil well; where you are growing; and at what stage of growth your plants are at. The general rule is... water when the soil needs it! While plants are growing, soil should always be moist to the touch but not sodden. If your soil is very wet – to the point that you could grab a handful and water would drip out – then there is no need to water until it feels just damp.

Get to know your soil: grab a handful of topsoil before watering, if it feels moist you can probably wait a day or two more before watering. Then dig down a little deeper (to around 10–15cm), how does that feel? For some soils like clay and loam it's likely the soil will be damper deeper down. But sandy soils can be moist on top and dry below the surface level, as moisture drains very easily.

Tiny seedlings and just-sown seeds will need watering regularly, especially if they are in direct sun or in a greenhouse. It will be worth checking these daily and watering daily or every other day until they establish good root systems.

Plants in pots are prone to drying out quickly. Check on even established veg plants in pots every day and water as required. Never leave plants in pots sitting in a pool of water for more than a day as this can cause the root systems to rot.

Taking cuttings

Cuttings are a great way to propagate new plants. They are most commonly taken as side shoots and stems, which are then placed into water or soil to grow roots. Cuttings are divided into a few categories, depending on when they are taken and at what stage of growth.

SOFTWOOD CUTTINGS

Softwood cuttings are taken from new, green growth in spring and early summer when the 'wood' (stem) is still be flexible and green. Softwood cuttings are great for perennial herbs such as sage and rosemary (pictured opposite) and can be also taken from annual plants such as tomatoes and basil.

Soft, green cuttings also do well when rooted in water. To do this, simply place the prepared cuttings in a glass of water, refreshing the water every few days until roots begin to appear (this can take a few weeks). Once roots appear, pot them up in individual pots to grow on.

- Using a sharp knife or pair of secateurs, cut off the growing tip of the plant (around 5–10cm), ensuring there are at least four sets of leaves running up the stem of the cutting you have taken.
- Cut again, just below the bottom set of leaves, doing so at an angle.
- Remove the bottom two or three sets of leaves by pinching them off.

- Push the prepared cuttings into pots of soil, making sure not to bury the leaves. I like to add a little sand and grit to cutting compost to aid drainage. For very soft stems you may need to make a hole with a chopstick first. You can place multiple stems in one pot by pushing the cuttings in a few centimetres apart from one another. It is best to take a few cuttings at a time as some may not root and will die off.
- Compost should be kept well watered with good drainage. Cuttings that are being grown on in soil should never sit in a pool of water as this will cause them to rot. Once the plants have rooted (usually in around three to six weeks) and put on new, green top growth, they are ready to be potted on.
- Take them out of their communal growing pots and pot each cutting up in its own 9cm pot. Once they reach around 10–15cm in height, pinch out the top growth to encourage branching and bushy new growth.

SEMI-RIPE CUTTINGS

Semi-ripe cuttings tend to be taken in summer and are also great for multiplying perennial herbs, such as all perennial mints. They are taken in much the same way as softwood cuttings: from the same year's plant growth, but when the stems are slightly more mature and the super-soft

green growth has started to become browner but remains pliable. Follow the softwood cutting process but stick to the soil technique as they are more likely to rot when rooted in water.

HARDWOOD CUTTINGS

The best time to take hardwood cuttings is just after leaf fall in autumn or just before budding in late winter. You're looking for the hard, brown wood that formed in the summer or in the previous year. Hardwood cuttings are great for fruit bushes such as currants and gooseberries. Fruit bushes need to be pruned in their dormant state to maintain their shape and productivity, so rather than discarding the prunings try turning them into cuttings to multiply your stocks.

- Take off 15–30cm lengths of cuttings, selecting vigorous-growing side shoots and stems. Cut just below a leaf node and snip off the growing tip to encourage rooting growth.
- Push the cuttings into a prepared bed in the ground, allowing 10cm between cuttings, or pot them up in the same way as softwood cuttings (see opposite). Do this in larger, deeper pots – pots that roses come in are great for this.
- Hardwood cuttings take a while to root so leave them be until the following summer/autumn. They can then be planted out in their final growing spot or in large containers.

Pruning

Pruning is the process of cutting branches, leaves or roots on a plant. It helps to remove dead plant material (which reduces the chances of infection), encourages new growth and gives the plant a better shape.

Knowing how and when to prune a particular plant is an art in itself. Like many areas of gardening, there isn't a 'one rule fits all' for pruning. Generally speaking, most herbaceous perennials, including many culinary herbs and most summer-flowering shrubs, produce shoots that flower in the same year. By contrast, most fruit bushes and trees produce flowers and fruits on last year's growth.

Cutting back woody material while a plant is dormant in winter usually promotes vigorous leaf growth in spring. Cutting leaf and branch growth in summer usually leads to more compact, controlled and shapely plants.

As a general rule of thumb, when pruning leafy perennials, always cut just above the leaf nodes on a stem. This will encourage bushy growth as the plant will create more stems above where it has been cut. This is also true for all things in the mint (*Lamiaceae*) family (most of our culinary herbs). Regular harvesting and pruning in

this way leads to much healthier, bushier plants.

Learning to prune is a tricky thing to do from a book. I recommend having some lessons from an experienced grower or checking out a few online tutorials to get the hang of it.

Pruning an apple tree

Pests and diseases

When we grow plants, particularly edible plants, we are manipulating nature. We clear weeds (take away food sources from wild insects and animals), clear around the edges of our plot (take away habitat) and attempt to produce the tastiest, juiciest fruits, leaves and tubers. It's no wonder that nature wants in. When we change natural environments to grow in a certain way, it can encourage pests and diseases to proliferate. The best treatment is prevention.

Create a garden that is a biodiverse ecosystem and it's less likely that one type of insect becomes a pest. Create habitats for beneficial predators, such as ponds for frogs and newts, as well as wildflower areas for invertebrates and dead wood piles for hedgehogs There will always be losses and successes at the hands of nature, but getting to know what you are up against and what non-toxic methods you can use to remedy problems will certainly aid your food-growing success.

A NOTE ON NEMATODES

Nematodes are tiny, microscopic biological warfare tools used to kill pests. They are parasites naturally present in the garden, meaning they are part of the ecosystem, but applied in high quantities they can be used for pest control. Nematodes tend to be specific to their host critters – in other words, if you buy nematodes to control slugs, they won't harm other bugs or wildlife.

Nematodes are available as a powder that you spray or water on to crops every few weeks. Applying nematodes at the right times, under the right conditions, can save an entire patch of baby lettuce or crop of carrots. They are expensive, though, which can be a limiting factor.

ALLIUM LEAF MINER

These feasters are the larvae of the allium fly and bore into the stems and bulbs of most allium crops, including leeks, onions, garlic and chives, chomping away and often opening the plant up to secondary infections, which can decimate entire beds.

The greyish brown flies are around 3mm long and can travel great distances. They first puncture the leaves and suck up the sap, leaving telltale lines of white dots on the foliage. They then lay their eggs, which hatch into small, white larvae. These cause the most damage as they tunnel through their host plant. Later in their life cycle, the larvae turn into brown pupae about 3mm long that are visible when the bulbs are cut.

Remedy Unfortunately, getting rid of allium leaf miner is tricky and there are no biological controls available. To help lessen the damage, cover allium crops with fine-mesh netting at peak laying times, which are April–May (mid- to late spring) and September–November (autumn). And always practise crop rotation (see p35) so that the bugs are less likely to overwinter in beds.

APHIDS

Aphids, also known as green or blackfly, come in a range of forms. They are small, sap-sucking insects and members of the family *Aphididae*. Over 5,000 kinds of aphid have been identified and hundreds of them commonly affect food crops. These tiny bugs reproduce at an alarming rate and tend to congregate around the buds and delicate growing tips of plants, sucking the sap and life force out of them as they multiply, leading to loss of flowers, fruits and leaves, and eventually killing the plant. Aphids need warmth to flourish so are generally found in the garden in summer. Indoor plants and those grown in greenhouses can be affected by aphids nearly year-round if not kept in check.

Remedy With a bit of care, aphids can be brought under control. Be sure to regularly check plants, especially those growing in a greenhouse. Manually squish large clusters of aphids with your fingers – not the nicest job, but it does work. Then after the bulk of them are removed, spray with soapy water: use 2 teaspoons of natural liquid soap to 500ml of warm water. Or try the all-round plant protection spray (see p150). Keep checking on infected plants and repeat the process two to three times a week until the infestation clears up.

BEET LEAF MINERS

Beet leaf miners are the larvae of small flies that eat between the layers of the leaves of beetroot and chard, leaving brown blotches and tunnels and weakening the plants. Beet leaf miner is most active between April and September.

Remedy Prune and remove leaves as soon as damage appears, or squash the mined blotches between your fingers to kill the larvae inside. If you have had a big infestation in previous seasons, practise crop rotation (see p35). Or try netting vulnerable crops with fine mesh early in the season.

BIRDS

Birds, mostly pigeons, can ransack a veg patch. They particularly like to munch leafy veg such as kale and chard. Leaves stripped back to the midrib is a telltale sign that pigeons have been at your crops. Pigeons and other birds will also pinch berries – strawberries, currants, raspberries, the lot!

Clockwise from top left Aphids on nasturtium flowers; aphids on a nasturtium leaf; aphids on feverfew flowers; lettuce suffering bird damage

Remedy The best way to stop birds is with physical barriers such as netting or twigs. For fruits and larger plants, as well as low-growing plants such as spinach, a cage is perfect, and you can drape this with netting (see p47).

BLIGHT
See tomatoes on p82.

BLOSSOM END ROT
Blossom end rot causes the ends of tomatoes and other *Solanaceae* family fruits to turn soft and black, making them inedible. It is caused by a calcium deficiency in developing fruit. Although soils usually have enough calcium in them, the problem is the plant's ability to make use of it. Soil that is too dry or too wet (often caused by fluctuations in watering) can lead to blossom end rot. Applying liquid feeds that are high in nitrogen while the soil is dry is also thought to block the plant's ability to take up calcium. Water regularly and apply liquid feeds while the soil is moist.

CARROT ROOT FLY
Carrot flies are small, black, flying insects whose larvae feed on carrots and related species, such as parsnips, celeriac and parsley. The larvae burrow into roots, leaving rusty brown holes and tunnels behind, opening affected vegetables up to secondary rot and leaving them inedible.

Remedy Sow carrot seeds sparsely to avoid having to thin them: it is thought

A tomato suffering from blossom end rot

thinning kicks up a carroty smell that the flies cannot resist. Practise crop rotation (see p35) so that the insects don't get too comfortable. Cover crops with fine-mesh netting to prevent flies from landing and laying their eggs. The most successful way to avoid or at least reduce carrot-fly damage is to use nematodes. Try *Steinernema feltiae* for spring applications and *S. carpocapsae* for summer applications. These can be bought separately, though most generic vegetable nematode mixes contain both.

CODLING MOTH
The larvae of these little moths bore into apples, eating them from the inside. They can also affect pears, plums, damsons and some nut trees. Codling moths begin nibbling their

way through fruits in midsummer, just as they are beginning to ripen. Often the fruits look perfect from the outside, with just a tiny brown exit hole that the larvae makes when it has had its fill. When you cut the fruits open, you see the damage in the form of brown tunnelling and caterpillar poop (aka frass). Delightful! Apples with codling moth damage cannot be stored. You can cut away undamaged parts for use in pies and cakes. The affect of the codling moth can be devastating, so it's worth getting on top of the problem fast!

Remedy Encourage natural predators of the larvae by placing bird feeders near apple trees. You can place pheromone traps in trees in early May. These attract male moths by imitating the scent of the female and trapping them on a sticky surface (it's mean, I know!). Spray codling moth nematodes (*Steinernema* spp.) in April and September/October to catch them in their larval stage.

CUCUMBER MOSAIC VIRUS

Cucumber mosaic virus (CMV) affects all members of the *Cucurbitaceae* family, including pumpkins, courgettes and cucumbers, and also attacks many other plants such as lettuce, spinach and flowers. It appears as yellow mottled patches on leaves and causes stunted growth. The virus is spread by some aphids, as well as by gardeners, gloves and garden tools. So always wash and disinfect anything that has touched an infected plant before touching healthy plants.

Remedy There are no known controls for CMV, but creating healthy, robust plants helps prevent infection taking hold. When choosing seed, go for strains bred to be CMV resistant. Keep aphids under control. And as soon as you spot signs of CMV, pull up affected plants and hot compost or dispose of them to stop the virus from spreading.

FLEA BEETLE

The flea beetle is a small, shiny, jumping insect of the leaf beetle (*Chrysomelidae*) family. It is often dark with a metallic hue but can come in a range of colours, from green to red. It is hard to spot, but one telltale sign of a flea-beetle infestation is hundreds of tiny holes nibbled in leaves. Some flea beetles even chomp away at the roots of crops. There are many kinds of flea beetle, each with its own favourite host plant, but in the edible garden they mostly affect brassicas, including radishes and rocket, as well as some *Solanaceae* genera such as *Capsicum* (peppers) and *Solanum* (aubergines).

Remedy Adult flea beetles overwinter in mulch, leaf litter, under rocks and in hedgerows. Some people recommend clearing these at the end of every year to reduce their hiding places. I find that an impossible task – and one that also damages the garden ecosystem, since

I purposely leave piles of leaves and mulch everywhere to create habitats for all kinds of creepy-crawlies. Instead of trying to clear every last fallen leaf from your garden, practise crop rotation (see p35). Companion planting can also help control flea beetle numbers: rows of dill, coriander, chamomile and catmint are thought to deter flea beetles by confusing them with odour. These flowering plants also attract beneficial insects that feed on the beetles, such as parasitic wasps. If the above fails, nematodes (see p141) are an effective biological control, particularly mixes containing a high percentage of nematodes from the *Steinernematidae* and *Heterorhabditidae* families.

PEA MOTH

A small, grey-brown moth whose caterpillars feed on peas. It usually goes unnoticed until it's time to shell the pods. The white larvae tunnel into peas, leaving behind a crumbly mess called frass (aka caterpillar poo). Luckily most pods only contain one or two affected peas so, with careful shelling, there is still a harvest to be had. The moths tend to only affect mature peas – growing flat-podded snow peas is one way to avoid them.

Remedy Practise crop rotation (see p35) as the larvae overwinter in the soil. You could cover pea plants with mesh nets, but this can be fiddly for tall, tendrilous plants.

Powdery mildew on a courgette leaf

POWDERY MILDEW

Powdery mildew is an incredibly common fungal disease that affects a huge range of plants, from calendula to cucumbers. It presents as white, dusty patches on the leaves and stems of plants and is caused by a number of different fungi that are specific to their host plant. The species that affects peas, for instance, is different from the one that attacks sunflowers. It isn't necessarily deadly to crops, but weakens plants, affects photosynthesis and results in a low harvest. Powdery mildew likes to hang out in warm, damp places, but confusingly often takes hold when plants have been subject to drought, as infrequent watering can weaken a plant's defences.

Remedy Combat by providing adequate spacing and airflow between plants. Once powdery mildew sets in, act fast and cut back affected leaves.

Bizarre as it sounds, try spraying the remaining, healthy leaves with diluted full-fat milk: one part milk to five parts water. Studies have shown this can be as effective as commercially available fungicides. Or try the all-round plant protection spray (see p150).

Most sources recommend destroying affected leaves as the spores of powdery mildew overwinter. But as it is so common and large amounts of green waste are affected by powdery mildew every year, I prefer to compost my infected leaves (in a very big, hot compost), using it to build my compost pile rather than chuck it in landfill or burn it. The choice is yours.

RUST

Rust is one of the most common forms of fungal disease found in the garden. It affects both edible and non-edible plants, including fruit trees, alliums and peas. It usually presents as flat or raised, yellow/brown spots on leaves

or stems of plants, but it can also affect flowers and fruits.

Remedy Cut away affected leaves as soon as rust appears. It is considered best to burn or throw infected leaves in the bin to prevent the spread of disease. As mentioned previously, I prefer to put them in the middle of a hot compost pile. Another remedy is to spray plants with bicarbonate of soda spray: 1 teaspoon bicarb to 500ml of warm water. This can help to stop rust if applied at the first signs of disease and used regularly.

SLUGS AND SNAILS

Of all of the common garden pests, slugs and snails are probably the most destructive. They can completely decimate entire plants or even beds of crops overnight under the right conditions. And they are not fussy, chomping their way through a wide range of edible and non-edible plants.

Remedy Most baby plants will need protection. Starting seeds off in modules under cover gives seedlings a chance to get bigger, stronger and make more bug-resistant plant chemicals to ward off slug attack.

Creating a barrier using crushed eggshells, coffee grounds or copper tape can be mildly effective at deterring slugs and snails, but does not work completely. Wool pellets (available online and from garden

Slug eggs in a pot of baby kale plants

The shiny, holey signs of slugs and snails

centres) make a better barrier when applied generously, but can be pricey, so shop around and buy them in bulk online. Don't skimp on application: allow a good 1cm deep and 10cm broad ring around vulnerable plants. What does work for me year on year is putting down nematodes every few months in wet, warm weather. The garlic spray (see p150) also makes a great deterrent.

I pick up slugs and snails by hand every few days after wet weather and feed them to the fish in my aquaponics system. Cardboard traps work a treat: simply lay some cardboard in crop beds and wait for the slugs to gather underneath, then, just before sundown, turn over the cardboard and collect the critters by hand.

Ducks are excellent slug hunters, so if you have space for them they are well worth the time and investment – not just for their creepy-crawly-hunting skills, but also for their delicious eggs.

SPIDER MITE

These are tiny (less than 1mm), sap-sucking mites that tend to affect greenhouse and indoor crops the most. They feed on a wide range of plants, including aubergines, peppers, cucumbers and figs, causing leaves and flower buds to shrivel and drop. The mites themselves are so tiny that they can be difficult to spot with the naked eye, but infected plants show a fine, insects that can help control spider mites, including *Feltiella acarisuga*, a predatory midge, and *Dalotia coriaria*, a spider mite-munching rove beetle. You can buy these biological controls online and release them into the affected growing area. But do not use in conjunction with the plant protection spray or any other insecticide sprays or you will lose your good bug army.

SQUIRRELS (AND OTHER SMALL RODENTS)

I grow in a garden surrounded by trees, and with trees come squirrels! Squirrels nibble at a variety of crops, including strawberries, bulbs, apples, beans, sweetcorn, nuts, sunflowers... the list goes on. I call squirrels the monkeys of Europe: they are cunning, fast and, relative to other pests, huge. They can really decimate crops.

Spider mites on an aubergine leaf

pale discolouration/mottling on the leaf surface and, in heavy infections, fine silk webs may be visible.

Remedy Spider mites thrive in warm, dry environments, so open greenhouse and polytunnel doors in the daytime and spray foliage with water to create a moist environment. Cut back severely infected leaves and use the plant protection spray every few days (see p150). There are a number of hungry, predatory

Remedy Netting can help deter squirrel damage, but because they are nimble and have little hands it is not always squirrel-proof. Stake down netting well with strong net pegs, leaving no gaps at all for them to slip under. One trick is to dust or spray vulnerable crops with a layer of chilli powder or spray (see p150): squirrels usually take one bite and never come back. You do have to wash your harvest thoroughly before eating it though, or you'll end up with spicy strawberries. The above remedies also help keep other small rodents at bay.

Plant protection sprays

These are some of my tried-and-tested protection sprays. They aren't foolproof, but they do help.

ALL-ROUND PROTECTION

I use this spray for a host of pests and diseases, including aphids, spider mite, powdery mildew and blight. Note that neem is a broad spectrum insecticide, so only spray this directly on problem areas or it may harm beneficial bugs.

• 2 teaspoons natural liquid soap
• 1 tablespoon neem oil
• 2 teaspoons bicarbonate of soda
• 500ml warm water

Mix the soap and neem oil to form an emulsion. Add in the bicarb and water. Place in a spray bottle. It keeps for a few weeks in a cool place. Shake well and spray directly onto infested areas.

GARLIC DETERRENT

This recipe can deter slugs, snails, aphids and caterpillars. It can also be useful for some fungal infections.

• 3–5 large garlic cloves
• 500ml warm water

Crush the garlic in a pestle and mortar and leave to sit for five minutes. Place the garlic and water in a large jar and shake. Leave this to sit for at least an hour or up to a few days. Strain out the garlic and pour the liquid into a spray bottle. Store in the fridge for a few weeks, but discard if mould begins to develop. Spray around the base of your plants and directly onto leaves after rain and on warm, wet evenings.

CHILLI SPRAY

This deters squirrels and other rodents.

• 2 tablespoons hot chilli powder
• 1 litre warm water

In a spray bottle, mix the chilli with the water. Shake well and spray over vulnerable crops. Caution: be aware of the wind direction when using this spray – a face full of chilli is no fun!

Harvesting

The harvest is the return for your care and attention. Treat it well for maximum reward.

CUT-AND-COME-AGAIN PLANTS

Cut-and-come-again is a method of harvesting that gives you a harvest and leaves the plant growing in the ground so that you can pick from it again (and maybe even again and again). It is best practised with leafy plants that grow in a basal rosette (a rosette/circular-shaped leaf arrangement growing from a central point). By cutting just the outer leaves of a plant growing in this pattern, you leave the central growing point intact to continue to grow. This kind of harvesting is suitable for rocket, lettuce, chicory, lamb's lettuce and many other leafy greens.

STORING YOUR HARVEST

Storing harvests in the correct way is very important to reap the full rewards of growing your own. Ideally you will eat as much as possible fresh from the garden when it is at its most tasty and nutritious, but sometimes there will be gluts.

Just like caring for your growing plants, each plant is different when it comes to storing. Below are a few general rules. Alternatively, you can always preserve your harvests, making jams, sauces, pickles, lacto ferments and dehydrated vegetable crisps or fruit leathers.

Potatoes, carrots and other starchy roots New potatoes don't store long and should be kept in the fridge. Maincrop potatoes and mature carrots can be kept in a cool, dark, dry place for months. You can pack/wrap in straw, just make sure the vegetables aren't touching.

Salads and leafy veg Leaves can be stored in a clip-lock box and kept in the

At the top, Chinese artichoke and mashua tubers; bottom right, oca tubers, and bottom left, Jerusalem artichokes

fridge for a few days. Wrapping them loosely in damp paper towels will make them last a little longer.

Tomatoes and peppers Both of these can last up to a few weeks in the fridge or a week or so in a cupboard, but are better cooked into sauces and frozen.

Courgettes and summer squash Store undamaged fruits in the fridge for weeks or sometimes even months, depending on the variety and maturity of the fruit.

Winter squash and pumpkins These can be left to 'cure' and can be stored for many months in a cool, dry, dark place. Again, you can pack in straw; just make sure they aren't touching each other.

Herbs Culinary herbs are always best fresh, but if you pick too much, simply pop the stems in a glass of water or wrap them in a wet paper towel and place in a clip-lock box in the fridge. They should last a few days or even a week or two if stored in this way.

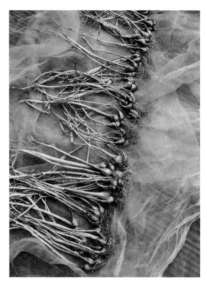

Garlic bulbs drying ahead of storage

Winter squash harvested for storing

Quarto

First published in 2024 by Frances Lincoln
an imprint of The Quarto Group.
One Triptych Place, London,
SE1 9SH
United Kingdom
T (0)20 7700 6700
www.Quarto.com

bloom
gardening · nature · inspiration

A Bloom book for Frances Lincoln
Bloom is an independent publisher for gardeners, plant admirers,
nature lovers and outdoor adventurers. Alongside books and stationery,
we publish a seasonal print magazine that brings together expert
gardening advice and creative explorations of the natural world.
Bloom celebrates all green spaces, from wilderness to windowsills,
and inspires everyone to bring more nature into their lives.
www.bloommag.co.uk | @bloom_the_magazine

Text © 2024 Vicky Chown
Photography © 2024 Aloha Bonser-Shaw
Cover illustrations © Botanical line art sketches by Madiwaso via Creative Market

Commissioning editor Zena Alkayat
Designer Sarah Pyke
Photographer Aloha Bonser-Shaw
Proofreader Joanna Chisholm
Indexer Hilary Bird

A catalogue record for this book is available from the British Library.

ISBN 978-0-7112-8137-0

Printed in China